The Art of Theory

THE ART
OF THEORY
Construction and Use

NICHOLAS C. MULLINS
Dartmouth College

HARPER & ROW, PUBLISHERS
New York   Evanston   San Francisco   London

To My Students

Standard Book Number: 06-044642-0

Library of Congress Catalog Card Number: 77-151332

Contents

Contents

Preface

This book has resulted from two years of teaching at Dartmouth College. It was written initially for a specific course, Sociology 8: Introduction to Social Analysis, one of the Dartmouth Sociology Department's four introductory courses. It has been designed for freshmen, sophomores, and others *without* prior training in the social sciences.

I want to thank James A. Davis, Chairman of Department of Sociology, Dartmouth College, for his many services in making this book possible. He has provided firm guidance by example and acid but accurate commentary on the major deficiencies of several drafts.

I do not have to find a cute way to thank my wife for services rendered in writing this book. She is my editor and critic. Her skill in reducing the elephantine prose of the original into this more readable version is appreciated beyond all telling. Linda Babbitt cared for my three children while my wife worked on the book.

Elsie Sniffin, the department secretary, has been most helpful in typing, running off copies of earlier drafts for student comments, and generally providing paper and good cheer for the enterprise.

Donna Musgrove has been a most competent and helpful typist.

The dedication to my students is in appreciation to those poor souls who, griping but with many helpful comments, struggled through early drafts of this manuscript, which was the prime text in a course, and who thereby made it a usable book.

N. C. M.

Chapter 1

INTRODUCTION

Social theory is neither magical nor new to today's students. You have been developing parts of a social theory ever since you first noticed that not all large human beings were "Mother." All the generalizations that have been made about how the social world operates (e.g., "All politicians are dishonest," or "People always look out for themselves") are part of this theory. It also includes the categories of people (e.g., friends, postmen, etc.) that you recognize in the world, and these simplify the necessity for dealing with hundreds of people every day of your life. These categories, plus the associated expectations about how people in them behave, order your understanding of society and give some assurance of predictability to the world.

When we think about ourselves, we recognize that we have complex, contingent (e.g., if he smiles, I'll smile) theories about social relations which we rarely verbalize or intellectualize. These theories are largely learned from experience, although some of their parts may have come from books, movies, discussions with others, and other secondary sources. Most of these theories are private and untestable. By keeping our theories private and unstated, we protect our human right to be perverse, limited, irrational, and inconsistent. Public statement of private theory is risky. We may be shown to be inconsistent, irrational, or just factually wrong, and this is bruising.

Social theory is the public statement of private theories about how society operates. If you examine the writings which constitute social theory, you will find them composed of complex, contingent statements about states of the social world and their interrelations. If you examine the books listed in the Bibliography, you will find many different forms of theory ranging from loose verbal discussions to strict formal presentations. These different forms represent different styles of public thinking about the complexities of the social world.

Social theory is difficult to communicate clearly. On one hand, we have sentences such as: "This is the dawning of the Age of Aquarius," or "I have a dream"; and, on the other, such statements as: "37 percent of all nonwhite families are headed by females." Some are intensely personal statements of vision; others are statements of fact needing a vision to order them. None of these three sentences will serve as a generally accepted public statement of a private theory, the first two because the statements contain no empirical aspect which can be checked against reality, the third because its generality is limited.

My approach to any theory will be pragmatic; its success or failure at explanation will determine whether we accept or reject it. I have not put theories into groups called "sociology" or "psychology"; consequently, we shall simply skip discussions of what "sociology" is and whether it is possible to "do" it.

In the course of this study you will be expected to do some theory. There are questions and exercises throughout the book, but these will only be trials of the special skills you will need to accomplish a larger task. That task is to develop analysis based on a theory about some aspect of social life. The exercises, rules and discussion are designed to lead you to *generate a simple system of empirically testable propositions* about social life.

Each of the emphasized words in the preceding sentence has special implications. To *generate* a theory, one starts with another theory, some experiences, and/or some general ideas or observations and combines them into something new. The following chapters provide simple rules for beginning to generate theory.

Simple theories (i.e., a few variables and a few simple connectives) are the easiest and, for reasons of space economy, the most sensible to study. Large, complex theories are compilations of small, simple theories and are not basically different.

A theoretical *system* differs from a guess, a result, or a single statement by being a set of statements that are related to one another. We will discuss ways to expand a few propositions into a system of propositions and to test that system for its connectedness.

An *empirically testable proposition* can be checked against reality. The best propositions are simple declarative sentences, for example, "Societies with high technical capabilities are interdependent." The propositions that we examine will be as general as this, and the style will be much the same.

My aim is to provide tools that will enable you to make your own theory testable and thereby to set real questions for research. The things you are trying to explain should come from your own experience, reading, or possibly a substantive course such as industrial sociology. Because this approach will bear fruit only if used in conjunction with research methods, I will sometimes suggest methodological techniques. The fine technical skills and manipulations necessary to develop complete tests of theories, however, can probably be best learned in research settings or a methods course. Theory taught apart from methods[1] provides only the means for asking interesting questions; only methods can help you find answers. The purpose of this book is to help you generate alternative theories which will form the basis for empirical questions.

This book can be described as *about* theory and not *of* theory. It should not be read apart from either (1) a substantive course in which real questions about the operation of

---

[1] The two are usually taught separately because (1) terms are short and (2) rarely do the same people want to teach both.

society are being asked, or (2) an introduction to sociology in which one is learning about society in general. It assumes that you have some experience and have done some reading. With each discussion of a particular technique are references to more detailed discussions and examples. The chapters conclude with exercises to test your skills. The general approach is open with respect to possible questions and sources of questions,[2] but rigorous at the point of synthesis and testing.

The use of others' material is a common practice in theory building. Even when a theory is written by one man, it is ultimately the product of many men. Theory building is a time-consuming and engrossing task when it is done with professional care and precision. It is quite beyond the capability of one man with his limited resources of time, energy, vision, and patience to build a complete, tested, and useful theory from scratch. Even with assistants to contribute their time and energy, the task is too large. Social scientists often work in groups of various sizes. They communicate quite freely with other scientists doing work in which they are interested. They also read the works of others, both alive and dead. A study is not considered complete, even if an investigator thinks he understands the problem under study, until the research is written up. The communication of scientific results and their acceptance by others is the crucial test of science. Almost anyone can provide a vision, but some visions order the experience of others.

This introductory text suggests ways to relate statements and draw conclusions from them. This method is best learned by actual trial and error. Specifically, you will need to develop a social theory from some statements about the world, and you will need to test your theory.

Why take this risk? Why learn any social theory? Most sociology students will not become professional sociologists or even use social theory obviously or directly (e.g., as social

---

[2] Students, particularly in an introductory course, are not generally aware of the literature in a field, but lecture material, textbooks, assigned readings, outside reading, and their own experience can provide potential parts of a theory.

workers or teachers). Nevertheless, every possible position in this or any other society will require you to make decisions about your activities as they relate to other individuals and social institutions. You will make these decisions with respect to your own social theory, good or bad, clear or muddled.

Social theory provides a powerful framework for seeing beyond the day-to-day concerns of newspapers to those processes that are working either to maintain or to change this world. I assume that you will not be exposed to much work by professional sociologists, and I have, therefore, not included much that is of strictly professional interest. We shall, instead,

1. develop rules for the clarification and systematization of thought and observation about society;
2. do some analysis to provide at least a minimum of experience;
3. consider how your theory and its assumptions might be tested and refined;
4. consider theory structure and its relations to empirical reality.

Figure 1.1 Organization of the Book

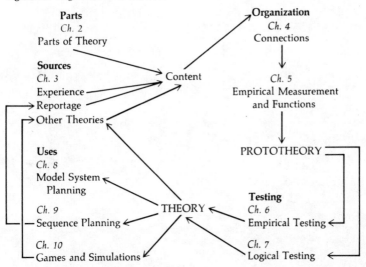

You can fill in your own content at every opportunity, and there will be many opportunities to do so.

Figure 1.1 shows how this book proceeds. Chapter 2 inventories the major parts of theory (i.e., concepts, variables, and relations). Chapter 3 suggests sources for the material with which you can begin building your own practice theory. With the help of techniques suggested in Chapters 2 and 3, you will do a partial inventory of ideas in the stocks of those persons or groups whose ideas you decide to use. Chapter 4 discusses the organization of theory parts through connecting statements of various types (rules, relations, and functions). In Chapter 5 we will consider the process of measurement and sampling in theory development. By this point you will have exhausted the material from your sources and developed a prototheory, an ordered collection of previously existing ideas. Chapters 6 and 7 consider empirical and logical testing respectively. (Any prototheory requires some logical and empirical testing before it can become a theory.) Chapters 8, 9, and 10 suggest different ways to use your theory. Chapter 8 introduces model system planning; Chapter 9, sequence planning; and Chapter 10, games and simulations.

Chapter 2

THE PARTS OF THEORY

Theories provide a bridge between language and experience. The two major parts of theory are *concepts*, a part of language, and *variables*, a summary of experience. A theory uses concepts and variables plus various other assorted parts to span the gap between what we know as ideas and what we perceive as experience. A concept consists of (1) an idea and (2) a word associated with that idea in some language (e.g., a common language such as English; a technical language such as sociology; or a formal language such as FORTRAN). A variable is a set of classifications to which experiences may be assigned.

CONCEPTS

A concept begins as an idea expressed in words; Chapter 3 suggests sources of these ideas. Since theories are about concepts, you must first decide what ideas are sufficiently important to form the basis for your concepts. If, to take an example, you are studying cooperation and conflict among races, an examination of your references will probably extract ideas such as "races," "occupational levels," "marriage," "classes," "integration," "separatism," "racism," and so on, some of which may ultimately not prove to represent basic concepts. If you are developing a theory about "football ability," "grades,"

7

and "attitudes," however, your theory must include at least these three ideas.

But an idea expressed in words is only the beginning of a concept. As we will see in the next chapter, each word exists within a network of other words (those which define it and those assumed to be synonymous or antonymous) which help to set its meaning; and meaning is further affected by context, group usage, and other factors which distinguish among words and their appropriate use.

The *idea* called to mind by a word is much more important than the word itself. These ideas are of two sorts: (1) examples of the word that one has seen or thought about; (2) those things which come to mind along with any particular example. When we "free associate," both sorts of ideas can occur without restriction. As scientists, however, our goal is to employ a specific abstraction which will bring the same ideas to the minds of a specific set of people. We occasionally disagree as to which of several words is more useful; the word itself, however, is less important than the context of words and experiences implied by it.

This core idea, which can be expressed in several related ways, constitutes a *concept* as we will use the term. Concepts can be expressed in terms of empirical definitions or of other concepts. For example, a concept which we express as "education" has a set of subconcepts: elementary education, trade education, continuing education, higher education, and so on; each of these more specific concepts is connected both to the more general concept and to a specific case (class) of a variable. In principle it is possible to have many layers of subconcepts between the most general concept under consideration and its related variable (for example, "shop" is a subconcept of "trade education"); in this book, however, we will limit ourselves to two levels: a general concept and several, more specific, subconcepts. Any general concept can be divided into subconcepts, and most sets of subconcepts can be collected into a more general concept, although not always usefully.

Concepts as you find them are often *raw*; that is, they are one of a series of ideas that may not be very clearly defined.

Refined concepts, by contrast, have mutually exclusive and totally inclusive partitions of the concept into a set of subconcepts. A set of subconcepts constitutes one partition of the concept. The above division of "education" suggests one partition of that concept; another might include "discussion," "lectures," "laboratory practice," and "reading" as subconcepts. You will want to use refined concepts and just one partition at any time. "Education," for example, should not be divided into "seminars," "trade education," and "books" since these subconcepts overlap and empirical analysis would therefore be inconclusive.

NECESSARY PROPERTIES FOR GENERAL CONCEPT SETS

Since theories are not about one concept, but rather sets of general concepts, we should consider the properties of these sets. One such property is *commonality*. Each concept applies to a specific range of real or potential empirical situations. If all concepts in a set apply to the same range of situations, the set has high commonality and can more easily be tested empirically (e.g., "education," "occupation," "political party preference," and "automobile preference" are all usable concepts for describing citizens of the United States; any sample of these citizens could provide a test of a theory using these concepts). A low-commonality set might include "length of men's lace cuffs" and "width of mastodon teeth."

You can achieve high commonality but have quite *uninteresting* concepts, a difficulty which can sometimes be remedied. A seemingly uninteresting concept may fit into a theory which already contains some intrinsically interesting or useful concept(s) (e.g., almost any concept would gain interest if it belonged to a theory which had "the probability of nuclear war" as another concept). Or it may fit a theory central to some field and therefore be interesting to some specific group of professionals. Concepts may also become interesting for very pragmatic reasons: Someone else is interested in them and may be providing financial support or other motivation for the research.

A concept may be interesting and common but still lack *clarity* with reference to other terms with which it is used. Each term's place in the language must be made as clear as possible. At this point the *community* which you are addressing becomes quite important, and this may be quite different from your personal community. If the generation gap holds, you and I do not share a language; in order to communicate with me, you may have to modify your language, and I, mine. For example, a social scientist is often writing for an audience of fellow professionals, and he will therefore use terms and phrases common to that body, such as "group" or "institution," which may or may not be what you think they are.

It might be helpful to keep a personal dictionary which records the meaning of various terms as defined by your own community.

RULE 2.1   Concepts may be subdivided into more specific concepts or collected into more general ones.

RULE 2.2   *a)* Concepts in the same theory ought, in principle, to be able to occur together; if they cannot, combine or divide them.

   b) Some of a theory's concepts ought to interest someone.

   c) Concepts should be clear and understandable by the intended audience.

EXAMPLE. If I were writing for an audience of high school teachers, my concepts might include:

1. "Class size" divided into "too small to provide variation," "too large to control," and "adequate";
2. "Form of lesson" divided into "rote learning," "projects," "drills on skills," and "gimmicks";
3. "Content" divided into "hard," "easy," and "acceptable."

For the school board these concepts might be divided differently: The class size might be expressed as "above present teacher-student ratio," "at present level," or "below"; the form of lesson in terms of "needs extra help or equipment," or "does not need extra help or equipment," and so on.

VARIABLES

A variable is a set of classifications into which empirical experiences or reports may be placed. We may associate names with these sets for convenience, but the way in which we classify these experiences is a much more important determinant of meaning. For example, we may have a set of classifications which we call "red, blue, green, and black," or "1, 2, 3, and 4." The meaning of these classifications, however, is settled not by the names, but rather by observing the placement of items (e.g., a puce carpet, a mauve chair) into these classifications. Each experience must be classified into one and only one classification of each variable. The purpose of classification is to generalize so that more than one experience will presumably belong in each classification. A graphic representation is given in Figure 2.1.

Figure 2.1 Variable Classifications of Experience

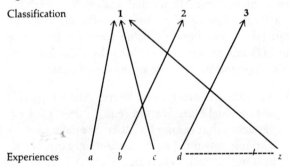

Rules for classification and measurement will be considered in Chapter 5. For the present you should note that each experience must be classified, and the number of classifications should be limited by determining either (1) the specific range (for example, a "length of time" variable could have the range "from 1 year to 10 years") or (2) the actual set of classifications (for example, "1 to 3 years," "4 to 6 years," "over 6 years").

TYPES

Variables come in several types. Those having a range of just two values (e.g., "male" and "female"; "in office" or "out"; "guilty" or "not guilty") are termed *dichotomies* and constitute the simplest form. (A one-class variable simply doesn't vary.) A dichotomy may be either natural (e.g., "male" and "female") or an investigator's attempt to simplify the world. The simplification will often be done by defining a positive case (e.g., "American citizen") and then assigning all other cases to an "other" value of the variable.

A second level of variables can include several well-defined, definite, and known values; "hair color," for example, can be "blond," "dark," and "other" (three classes) or "blond," "dark," "red," "white," "auburn," and "others" (six classes). In any case, a relatively small number of values for the variable exist. These sets of values may be natural ones, or they may be created by the investigator. They may also have an implied order (e.g., "infant," "young," "middle-aged," "old"); the hair color set has no such order.

A third group of variables is termed *scales*. If a variable (1) has such a large number of values that for *all practical purposes* it can take every possible value from the lowest to the highest and (2) has an implied order to the classifications, it forms a scale. Age and income are examples of scales.

RULE 2.3 *a)* Variable sets must be *inclusive*. Always specify one residual classification (e.g., "other") for experiences that cannot be otherwise defined.

        b) Variable sets must have *one* and only one classification for each experience.

RULE 2.4 State both your variables and your concepts in dichotomous form during the early stages of theory building.

EXAMPLE.
Concept: Experience
Variable: Length of time on the job
Three possible forms of the variable:

1. *NUMBER OF YEARS*

   Measurement: Question: When were you hired?
   Present date — answer to above = value of variable.
   Range: 0 to the most years in organization, certainly under 100.

Or

2. *COHORTS* (persons who entered the organization within the same ten-year period)

   Measurement:

Date Hired	Value of Variable
1900–1910	0
1911–1920	1
1921–1930	2
1931–1940	3
1941–1950	4
1951–1960	5
1961–1970	6
1971–Present	7

   Range: 0 to 7

Or

3. *NEW OR OLD*

   Measurement: Question: Were you hired before 1960?

Answer	Value of Variable
yes	old
no	new

   Range: old or new.

DEFINITIONS

So far we have discussed variables (e.g., "length of time" in three possible classification forms) and concepts (e.g., "experience," defined as "length of time on the job"). These two entities are joined in the theory-building process by a definition. A variable is a *potential empirical proxy* for a concept. It summarizes measurements of an attribute of a situation or thing. It must be a *proxy* because a concept cannot be directly measured but is rather associated with a variable that can be measured. It is a *potential* proxy because a variable must be explicitly associated by a definition with a concept before it can become that concept's proxy. Definitions are of two types: procedural and verbal.

PROCEDURAL DEFINITIONS

If you have a concept with several subconcepts and you wish to classify a series of individuals, you need a variable. For example, take the concept "education," divided into the subconcepts "grade school education," "high school education," and "college education." These can be measured only by using some *procedure* which will relate each subconcept to one and only one classification of a variable. Suppose you have measured the number of school years completed for a population. You then have a variable that has as classifications the counting numbers: 0, 1, 2, 3, . . . , 12, 13, 14, . . . , 20, 21, . . . , etc., plus a residual classification ("no answer," "other," "did not understand question," etc.). For simplicity call it 28 classifications, 0–26 years and "other." The next step is to map this variable onto the three subconcepts. One simple way to do this is to classify answers between 0 and 8 inclusive, or "other," as "grade school"; answers between 9 and 12 inclusive as "high school"; if over 12, as "college." This procedure maps every classification of the variable onto one subconcept.

VERBAL DEFINITIONS

A verbal definition moves from a variable to a concept. If you begin with a variable such as the 28 classifications utilized above, you will want to know what concept this variable potentially indicates. Concepts that might possibly be associated with this variable are: experience, length of service, education, exposure, and so on. A dictionary and/or synonym list might help clarify exactly which concept to use. In creating the definition, take care to describe the variable in terms that will clearly indicate the specific concept to which you are relating it.

In trying to develop a verbal definition, you may find that a variable doesn't relate to any concept of any importance to your theory, in which case you should forget the variable. When using verbal definitions, you must balance the costs of getting data for those variables that exactly describe the concept in which you are interested against the theory's lessened importance if you conceptualize your variables narrowly. (For example, the variable "years in school" could be narrowly conceptualized as "time spent in an educational institution." A broader conceptualization of this variable would be "education.") Since the first cost is in dollars and the second difficult to measure, researchers have tended to conceptualize narrowly; the result has generally been trivial concepts and noncomparable results.

Concepts are not free floating; they cannot be assigned freely to any variable. They are embedded within networks of implication and meaning no matter how they are represented (e.g., as words or other symbols). Had you assigned the concept "intelligence" (instead of education) to the variable discussed at the beginning of this section, you would be questioned.

USING DEFINITIONS

As you examine your collected material, you will find that some sources have not produced concepts for the variables they measure while others give no procedures for their concepts. Several strategies are open to you at this point, each dependent on where you are in your research. I am assuming that, as a beginner, you will be using other people's data and generating your own theory. For you, then, variables are relatively fixed; you must search for adequate concepts. One example will illustrate this situation. If you wanted to examine the number of years of school completed by the whole American population, you would most likely use U.S. Census data. You may manipulate the Census figures to some degree, but you are limited to those variable classifications used by the Census; you must use "number of years completed in school" as the variable, not "information gained" or some other measure. Were you planning your own study, your choice of variables would be much freer.

When taking variables from someone else's work, you may find by examination that two or more fit naturally with one or more of the concepts you have already defined. If you have two indicators for the same concept, use both in order to reduce your chances for error. The matching of concepts and variables in definitions will also force you to make some crucial decisions. What is your theory about? If some variables do not attach to important concepts within your theory, you will probably want to set those variables aside.

Your concepts should also be considered. Do they have procedures? If not, do any of the variables indicate, however weakly or indirectly, the status of those concepts? Suppose, for example, that you are examining data and a theory about differences in medical care based on social class. You are not given income or occupational information, but you do know the number of school years completed. Although the education measure will be a poor proxy, you know that in American society education and class are generally closely related. You may decide, therefore, to let the number of school years completed indicate social class. If even this fails, the concept should be dropped since at this point you are probably not prepared to design and execute a new data-gathering project.

Beyond these concerns, definitions must meet a validity criterion; that is, your definition must be accepted by some competent other person as a proper indicator of the concept and a proper conceptualization of the variable.

You may sometimes discover that a concept is little more than the variable specifications put into words. On other occasions you may find the reverse: a very narrow variable paired with a very general concept. If you were to use the price of candy in one hundred stores as a variable for the general concept "all retail prices," I would object to the difference in scale between the concept and the variable. You might try to remedy this deficiency by indicating *how* a smaller concept (e.g., candy prices) is actually being given a procedural definition and how this smaller concept links to the larger. (Candy prices are clearly a small part of retail prices.) You can link the concept "candy prices" with the concept "retail prices" because we do expect the price of candy and the total retail price index to be related (although not perfectly).

Even in the professional literature, not every concept/ variable pair provides a good example of adequate definition. Nevertheless, the need for good procedural and verbal definitions is one reason the beginning student theorist should start with an existing theory or propositional inventory even though this rule limits, at least initially, the range of variables and concepts he can select. Until the student has some experience, he should use definitions from sources as much as possible. Beware of easy conceptualization.

Variable formulations must have built into them the power to discriminate between instances, and concepts must have subconcepts. Every definition must include points at which every level of discrimination in a variable relates to one and only one subconcept of the related general concept. Figure 2.2 shows the general pattern; specific examples will be presented later.

Figure 2.2 Concepts and Variables

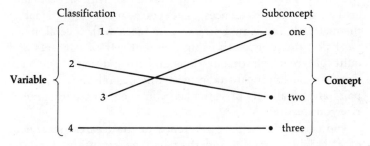

The pattern for definitions is quite simple: Each classification of a variable must be matched to one and only one subconcept of the associated concept. This pattern can be symbolized graphically (as in Figure 2.2), verbally, or by formula. Such precise definitions are absolutely essentially to good theory.

To summarize:

RULE 2.5 Use definitions from your sources until you are experienced in handling definitions. Beware of easy conceptualizations.

RULE 2.6   In a definition, match each classification (value) of a variable to one and only one subconcept of the associated concept by means of graphic, verbal, or mathematical statement.

EXAMPLE.

	Classifications	Subconcepts	
	Chromosome configuration		
Variable	XX XY Any other	Female Male Other	Associated Concept: Sex

A METHOD
FOR COLLECTING
REFERENCES

Suppose you were suddenly handed a block of reading material (after having asked someone familiar with a particular area to give you references), and you wanted to systematize the material. You would probably be faced with several major works on the topic, each using different sets of concepts and quite different sets of questions and assumptions. You may have several empirical studies with findings relevant to specific pairs and small sets of variables; you need a way to summarize your reading.

File cards with a page reference to the clearest statement of a variable, concept, and their linkage are useful for later double-checking. On the front of the card list a variable giving the specific place, time, and group with which this variable has been observed. (Be gullible about data until you start finding contradictions.) A general format for the front might look like Figure 2.3, Front.

The back of the card should show the associated concept with its subconcepts; a general, verbal definition; a page reference to a clear definition of the concept; and cross references to other concepts related to this one. A format for the back might look like Figure 2.3, Back.

A second card containing each assertion by an author of a

Figure 2.3 Dummy Card Layouts: Format

Front

Variable	Observed Time: Group: Place:	Page Reference:
Classifications	Observations	

Back

Concept:		Page Reference:
Verbal def:		
Subconcepts	Variable Classes	
Cross references:		

relation between concepts is also helpful. If the assertion is part of a short quote, record the quotation.

Using this format, one can gradually build a file for any book or set of books. If you were reading Clifford Geertz, *The Religion of Java*, you would find the following text on page 110:

> Sorcery, then, as the Javanese conceive of it, tends to be practiced on neighbors, friends, relatives and other acquaintances fairly close at hand.

This statement associates at least two items: sorcery and the persons who are objects of sorcery. You could use the card format to record variables and concepts as in Figure 2.4. The passage indicates that a (+) on distance (close relations) "goes with" a (+) on sorcery (more frequently practiced). If you find a more precise statement of functions (for example, a correlation coefficient), note that fact on the card.

You will find that concepts in social theories are usually formulated very broadly. Since variables are necessarily more limited, social theorists often find it quite difficult to fit concepts with empirical variables. One attempt to "solve" this problem has been to insist that no concept have a wider range than the empirical variables with which it is associated. This rule is fine for a specific study, but it reduces very sharply the

Figure 2.4   Dummy Card Layouts: Filled In

Front: card 1

Distance:	1950s	Geertz
	Java	R. of Java p. 110
	Javanese	

Classification	Observation
(+)	Relatives, friends, neighbors, acquaintances
(−)	Others

Back: card 1

Social distance

Concept	Subconcept	Variable	Classification
Near		+	
Far		−	

(Figure 2.4 continued)

Front: card 2

Sorcery	1950s	Geertz
	Java	R. of Java p. 110
	Javanese	

Classification	Observation
1	Hiring
2	Suspecting others
3	No activity

Back: card 2

Sorcery

Concept	Subconcept	Variable	Classification
	Practice	(+)	1
			2
	Not	(−)	3

Card 3

Distance, Positive, Sorcery	Geertz
	R. of Java p. 110

generalizability of theory and prohibits abstractness. If we consider that the whole purpose of theory is to provide a clear intellectual picture which will promote understanding of the rich tapestry of reality, then we can see that limiting abstractness cripples a theory's ability to order broad ranges of material.

The aspects of abstractness that most concern beginning students are (1) the loss of detail in meaning and (2) the possibility of alternate linguistic formulations. For example, "education" means more than simply "number of years in school." (We all know people who sit in school and do not learn anything; few persons would define "sitting in school" as a proper education.) In taking a gross measure, we lose this detail in both the process and its final result in data. But we can agree that "number of years" has something to do with education and then suspend judgment on the adequacy of this definition as a measure. The real test of a definition's adequacy then becomes empirical. Does the variable behave as it should, given our theory? If it does not, the variable's inadequacy *may* be a reason.

You must also remember that language is rich in alternate empirical meanings for its words. When you use common language terms in a theory, specificity is necessary because you lack many of the contextual clues through which English indicates the intended meaning for any specific use. Common language words often express both concepts and variables. "Education," for example, can refer both to the *process* and the *product* of learning. To avoid empirical chaos you must define two concepts, "education 1" and "education 2," as is done in the dictionary, and designate one concept "the process of learning" and the other "the product of learning." Then you can associate two variables, "teacher-pupil communication measures" and "pupil test scores," with the first and the second respectively. You may subsequently associate "education 1" and "education 2" as "education 3." By specifying those aspects of a definition that you intend to consider empirically, you retain some of the word's English richness even though the concept itself is fairly abstract.

RELATIONS

To this point we have been building the "words" of a theory. These words are the concepts and variables connected by definitions. Having clarified the words of your theory for future usability, you are now ready to explore the relations which will cement those words into a theory.

An abstract empirical relation[1] states that two concepts are related because they are defined as connected or not connected to two variables that are nonrandomly associated. For example, "age" and "education" are related because any reasonable variables for these two concepts are nonrandomly associated. The simple fact of association is generally not very interesting.

An abstract empirical relation can have three subtypes: positive, negative, and none. To produce these *signed relations*, you must give an order to the subconcepts of your general concepts; in arbitrary fashion you assign a "—" or "+" to one end of the order and the opposite sign to the other. A positive relation between concepts indicates that identically signed values of the connected variables tend to be associated; a negative relation, that values tend to be opposite in sign; and no relation, that the variables do not relate in any systematic pattern. We can symbolize five cases of related dichotomous concepts (see Table 2.1).

Table 2.1 Symbolization of Dichotomous Concepts

Case	Concept 1	Concept 2	Sign of Relation	Symbol
I	+	+	+	————
II	+	—	—	- - - -
III	—	+	—	- - - -
IV	—	—	+	————
V	No pattern (+ and —)	No pattern (+ and —)	0	

In analyzing concept relations you may find that several different relations between two concepts are actually proposed

---

[1] Relations could be of many types (logical, aesthetic, symbolic, etc.), but here we are interested only in abstract empirical relations.

at different places in the same work. You can then build several alternative theories and test them against each other. And you may also find that not every concept will be linked to every other.

In addition to sign, you can assert an asymmetric relation when one of the following conditions pertains or is assumed to pertain among the concepts:

1. One can produce the change in *y* with changes in *x* but not vice versa.
2. There need be no change in any other variable for *x* to affect *y* (*x* is sufficient to change *y*).
3. The two variables have an unambiguous time separation, *x* occurring first (e.g., high school grades and college achievement).
4. *x* is a more permanent or lifelong characteristic (e.g., race, sex), and *y* can change over time (e.g., political beliefs, religious affiliation).
5. *x* is stated as the "cause" of *y*.

After linking some of your concepts, say *x* and *y*, you can symbolize that *x* is asymmetrically associated with *y* (*x* precedes *y*), and not vice versa, either by writing a word sentence to that effect or by graphing and using arrows: "*x*→*y*," and not "*y*→*x*" (see Table 2.2). This notation indicates simply

Table 2.2 Sentences to Symbolization

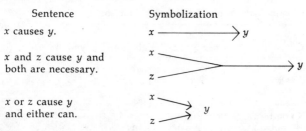

Sentence	Symbolization
x causes *y*.	*x* ⟶ *y*
x and *z* cause *y* and both are necessary.	*x*, *z* ⟶ *y*
x or *z* cause *y* and either can.	*x*, *z* → *y*

that "*x*," a generalized name for one concept, and "*y*," the generalized name for another concept, are related such that, subject to the rules below, a change in the value of *x* is associated with a change in the value of *y*. You will find some proposed relations that do not fit any of these rules. You will find others explicitly labeled as situations in which the two concepts are related but not in any causal way. Both are symbolized by the signed but directionless lines discussed above (e.g., "x- - - -y"; translates x and y are negatively related). If you are not certain which case you have, I suggest that you produce one model containing the first alternative and a second containing the other.

These relations are basically asymmetric, signed associations between pairs of concepts graphed to show all known connections among the set of concepts under consideration. Using these relations we can consider a detailed example showing how concepts, variables, definitions, and relations are used, but first let us summarize:

RULE 2.7 *a*) If you think two concepts are associated, draw a graph linking them. Not all pairs of concepts need be linked.

   b) If the identically signed subconcepts of two concepts tend to be associated, then link the two concepts with a positive relation (solid line). If differently signed, link them negatively (broken lines).

RULE 2.8 We assert an asymmetric relation when one of the following conditions pertains or is assumed to pertain:

   a) One can produce a change in y with changes in x but not vice versa.

   b) There need be no change in any other variable for x to affect y (x is sufficient to change y).

   c) The two variables have an unambiguous time separation, x occurring first (e.g., high school grades and college achievement).

   d) x is a more permanent or lifelong characteristic (e.g., race, sex), and y can change over time (e.g., political beliefs, religious affiliation).

   e) x is stated as the "cause" of y.

EXAMPLE

I will first reproduce a discussion of organizations from Berelson and Steiner's *Human Behavior:* An Inventory of Scientific Findings (1964, pp. 363–364, 369–370). This particular book simplifies theory building by placing many terms in definition form and setting out propositions. In effect, this and other propositional inventories are ready-made collections of findings similar to those you are making for your own theory.

ORGANIZATIONS

In recent years sociologists have become more and more interested in the study of organizations. But however active the work, it is perhaps fair to say that the concern has been expressed primarily in conceptualizations, theoretical formulations, and a few case studies; it has not yet eventuated in a major body of findings established by hard scientific evidence. This explains, in part, why such a burgeoning field is represented here by a relatively small set of findings. . . .

As for the importance of the topic itself, it is perhaps necessary only to quote the introductory words of a recent book by two authorities in the field:

Organizations are important because people spend so much of their time in them. . . . In our society, preschool children and non-working housewives are the only large groups of persons whose behavior is not substantially "organizational" [March and Simon, 1958, p. 2].

In daily life, of course, organizational behavior is interwoven with face-to-face and institutional relations; for our purposes, however, it can be treated separately in this way.

DEFINITIONS

Organizations: A standard book in this field begins by saying that "it is easier, and probably more useful, to give examples of formal organizations than to define the term. The United States Steel Corporation is a formal organization; so is the Red Cross, the corner grocery store, the New York State Highway Department" (March and Simon, 1958, p. 1). According to another specialist, "An organization consists of a number of people, formally joined together and usually assigned specific functions, for the purpose of achieving a stated goal" (Sills, 1962).

Among the types of (formal or complex) organizations that might be cited by way of exemplification are business firms, military units, churches, hospitals, clubs and lodges, colleges and universities, political parties, prisons, and labor unions. Besides their specialization by field of activity, what do such organizations have in common? The major characteristics are these:

Formality: An organization typically has an explicitly formulated set of goals, policies, procedures, rules and regulations that define appropriate behaviors for its members.

Hierarchy: An organization typically has a pyramidal arrangement of power and authority with more or less clearly demarcated levels. Some people are higher in the organization than others and hence have some authority over what the others do as members of the organization. As a rough rule of thumb, an organization has at least three levels of authority.

Size and/or complexity: An organization usually contains more than just a few people; usually the membership is large enough so that close personal relations among all are impossible. (Strictly speaking, some small and simple groups can be called organizations—the corner grocery store cited above or the doctor's office with a medical technician, nurse, and stenographer—but usually something more substantial than that is meant.) Hence, there is a certain impersonality about the organization's actions or dealings with its public, and this is where the normal connotation of bureaucracy comes in.

As a matter of fact, in much of the sociological literature the terms "bureaucracy" and "organization" are synonymous, or virtually so (and "bureaucracy" is by no means limited to governmental organizations).

Duration: An organization typically exists longer than the lifetime or the affiliation of any particular member or leader. Thus a business firm, a university, a political party, a particular church will still be there fifty or a hundred years from now—with, of course, a completely new set of members. In most cases, organizations have some physical property to mark them off—a plant, an office, a campus, an army base, a hospital and so on.

. . .

A4 The more physically decentralized the organization with administrative autonomy given to the units, the more different and often discordant understandings and points of view there will be within the organization, and the more they will be tolerated.

Similarly, the more channels of communication there are within an organization, the greater will be the discrepancy among the members' understandings and points of view. Actually, decentralization is one means of containing deviance within a single over-all organization, and this makes for the survival of the whole.

A4.1 The more decentralized the organization, with lower units autonomous yet visible to higher ones, the better the identification of the members with the organization is likely to be.

One reason for this is the individual's better chance to be taken into account in a decentralized situation: smaller pond, bigger frog.

In one well-known experiment in industry the degree of centralization was systematically varied. In two offices there was close supervision over subordinates, in two similar offices there was delegation of authority. After a year, the more centralized office had higher productivity, but the decentralized one had better morale. . . .

In a study of a national health organization, decentralized control over the spending of funds helped to keep up the vitality of the local units (Sills, 1957).

A4.2 An organization is more likely to be strongly centralized during external crises than during normal periods.

Thus military organizations are more centralized than most other types, and they are closer to crisis conditions:

The greater the imponderables and uncertainties that military command has to face, the more emphasis is placed on explicit orders, elaborate directives, and contingency plans [Janowitz, 1959, p. 83].

A5 A period of innovation and change affecting an organization is likely to produce a heightened amount of communication among the members, communication oriented both toward the task and toward mutual emotional support.

A6 The communications down the organizational hierarchy are likely to be critical, and the communications up the hierarchy are likely to be commendatory.

Bad relations in the line of command will result in poor communication. Gardner has described the way in which members of social organizations are nervously looking upwards while their superiors assess them, and how bad news is held up or distorted in order to keep the good opinion of those higher up. . . . In a laboratory experiment on groups with status divisions, Kelley (1951) found low-status members more ready to communicate upwards about irrelevant matters, and unwilling to criticize high-status members [Argyle, 1957, pp. 190–91].

A6.1 The more rigidly or formally organized the hierarchy, the less the upward flow of informal communications.

For example, this is particularly evident in the military, because of its sharp distinctions by rank. In a governmental agency, one study showed, subordinates consulted with one another about difficult decisions rather than with their supervisor, lest he interpret such consultation as indecisiveness or weakness (Blau, 1955).

A7 The efficiency of a large formal organization is sizably enhanced when its own chain of command or decision or communication is tied into the informal network of groups within the organization, so that the network can be used to support the organization's goals.[2]

For this example I will begin with eight concept-variable units: decentralization, similarity, tolerance, identification, communication, crisis, visibility, and channels. For four of these I will give the concept name and dictionary definition, a verbal definition, and a procedural definition followed by a variable name, the number of classifications involved, and the measurement procedure used. Last will be one short example of a case and how it was classified. The second four units you may complete as an exercise.

1. Decentralization
    a) *Concept:* (decentralize, v.t.) "to break up the centralization of authority, as in a government or industry, and distribute among more places, local authorities, etc." (p. 280).[3]
    b) *Verbal definition:* A count of decision centers indicates centralization or decentralization.
    c) *Procedural definition:* If more than one decision center exists within an organization, score "high decentralized." If only one, score "low decentralized." If there is no center, no information or other conditions, score as "other."
    d) *Variable:* number of decision centers; three classes:

[2] From HUMAN BEHAVIOR: AN INVENTORY OF SCIENTIFIC FINDINGS by Bernard Berelson and Gary A. Steiner, © 1964, by Harcourt Brace Jovanovich, Inc., and reprinted with their permission.

[3] This and all subsequent page referents in this chapter are to *Webster's New World Dictionary* (Springfield, Mass.: G. and C. Merriam Co., 1957).

respectively "high" (more than one), "low" (one), and "other."

e) *Measurement:* interviews with members of the organization about the making of previous decisions. Crucial question: "Were you able to make that decision we were talking about by yourself? If not, where was it made?" If the answers show that, for all classes within the organization, decisions to be made are referred to the same decision-making point, then there is one center. If they do not, there are several.

f) *Example:* a set of interviews made in a large corporation showed that all questions about hiring policies had been settled in the personnel department. For personnel, then, this was a centralized company.

2. Similarity
   a) *Concept:* (similar) "nearly but not exactly the same or alike; having a general resemblance" (p. 1359).
   b) *Verbal definition:* the percentage of similar viewpoints expressed, with a range from 0 to 100, indicates one kind of similarity.
   c) *Procedural definition:* "high similarity" exists if expressed opinions are the same and are thought to be the same. "Medium" if opinions are the same but this similarity is not noted by those within the organization. "Low" if the opinions of more than 25 percent of the people in the organization differ from those of the rest. All others code "dissimilar."
   d) *Variable:* expressed opinions; four classes: "high," "medium," "low," "dissimilar" (includes "others").
   e) *Measurement:* interview questions about policy agreement in the organization. Specifically, do people in this organization generally agree on policy matters?
   f) *Example:* one executive reported "market stability" as the "primary goal of the organization"; another suggested "maintaining market share." They both were coded "high agreement" when they also stated that most people thought that this was the policy.

3. Tolerance
   a) *Concept:* (tolerate) "to recognize and respect others' beliefs, practices, without necessarily agreeing or sympathizing" (p. 1532).
   b) *Verbal definition:* the percentage of negative reactions to disagreement might indicate tolerance.
   c) *Procedural definition:* if there are 10 percent or more negative reactions of disagreement, then score "not tolerant." If no negative reactions or no information is given, score "tolerant."
   d) *Variable:* sanctions; two classes: "not tolerant" and "tolerant" (includes all others).
   e) *Measurement:* when, in the course of an interview, a negative response to an act of disagreement is reported, score 1. Take the number of such incidents over all incidents of disagreement and report.
   f) *Example:* "I knocked him out"; score 1. Two similar responses out of a possible 20 would score "not tolerant."

4. Identification
   a) *Concept:* "3. to join or associate closely; as 'He has become identified' " (p. 721).
   b) *Verbal definition:* the way in which an organization's members refer to it indicates identification with it.
   c) *Procedural definition:* if, in the course of a selected half hour of conversation, all references to the organization are phrased as "we," then score "high identification." If more than half but not all are to "we," then score "low." All others score "not identified."
   d) *Variable:* verbal identification; three classes: "high," "low," "not."
   e) *Measurement:* half-hour conversation, interviewer noting how interviewee refers to his organization.
   f) *Example:* "We won that game." Two such references out of a possible three would score "low."

The following section restates rules and suggests exercises. At the end of each chapter I will summarize the rules stated during the chapter and, where useful, provide exercises that will test your understanding of the work to that point.

RULES

RULE 2.1 Concepts may be subdivided into more specific concepts or collected into more general ones.

RULE 2.2 *a*) Concepts in the same theory ought, in principle, to be able to occur together; if they cannot, combine or divide them.

b) Some of a theory's concepts ought to interest someone.

c) Concepts should be clear and understandable by the intended audience.

RULE 2.3 *a*) Variable sets must be *inclusive*. Always specify one residual classification (e.g., "other") for experiences that cannot be otherwise defined.

b) Variable sets must have *one* and only one classification for each experience.

RULE 2.4 State both your variables and your concepts in dichotomous form during the early stages of theory building.

RULE 2.5 Use definitions from your sources until you are experienced in handling definitions. Beware of easy conceptualizations.

RULE 2.6 In a definition, match each classification (value) of a variable to one and only one subconcept of the associated concept by means of graphic, verbal, or mathematical statement.

RULE 2.7 *a*) If you think two concepts are associated, draw a graph linking them. Not all pairs of concepts need be linked.

b) If the identically signed subconcepts of two concepts tend to be associated, then link the two concepts with a positive relation. If differently signed, link them negatively.

RULE 2.8 We assert an asymmetric relation when one of the following conditions pertains or is assumed to pertain:

a) One can produce a change in y with changes in x but not vice versa.

b) There need be no change in any other variable for x to affect y (x is sufficient to change y).

c) The two variables have an unambiguous time separation, x occurring first (e.g., high school grades and college achievement).

d) x is a more permanent or lifelong characteristic (e.g., race, sex), and y can change over time (e.g., political beliefs, religious affiliation).

e) x is stated as the "cause" of y.

EXERCISES

1. Analyze the concepts "communication," "crisis," "visibility," and "channels" as used by Berelson and Steiner in the material reproduced above and defined below.

a) *Communication:* "a giving or giving and receiving of information signals or messages by talk, gesture, writing, etc." (p. 296).

b) *Crisis:* "a turning point in the course of anything; decisive or crucial time, stage, or event. 3. a crucial situation, situation whose outcome decides whether possible bad consequences will follow, syn. emergency" (p. 349).

c) *Visibility:* "2a the relative possibility of being seen under the conditions of distance . . . prevailing at a particular time" (p. 1630).

d) *Channel:* "5. any means of passage; course through which something moves or passes. 6. The proper or official course for transmitting communications . . ." (p. 244).

Use the format for "decentralization" as an example.

2. Take three concepts; decide what variables would be good indicators for them. Describe the range or classification of values for these variables.

BIBLIOGRAPHY

BLALOCK, HUBERT M. *Theory Construction: From Verbal to Mathematical Formulations.* Englewood Cliffs, N.J.: Prentice-Hall, Inc., 1969.

An essentially similar view of the process of building theory from verbal statements to more rigorous formulations of theory. Highly technical, requires multiple regression techniques to understand.

BUNGE, MARIO. *Scientific Research.* New York: Springer-Verlag, 1967.

An attempt at a systematic technical philosophy of science. More readable than most. Contains problems, bibliography and is well written.

GREER, SCOTT. *The Logic of Social Inquiry.* Chicago: Aldine, 1969.

A book full of good suggestions, but not very well focused.

HOULT, THOMAS FORD. *Dictionary of Modern Sociology.* Totowa, N.J.: Littlefield, Adams and Co., 1969.

A good attempt to define a series of terms in use in sociology and other closely related sciences. Hoult also lists terms that tend to occur together and cross-references heavily.

STINCHCOMBE, ARTHUR. *Constructing Social Theories.* New York: Harcourt Brace Jovanovich, Inc., 1968.

A very good example of building concepts and interrelating them. Also a good example of doing sociological theory.

ZIMAN, JOHN. *Public Knowledge: The Social Dimension of Science.* Cambridge: Cambridge University Press, 1968.

Starting from the view that the goal of science is a consensus of rational opinion over the widest possible field, Ziman discusses a nontechnical philosophy of science which emphasizes the social aspect.

Chapter 3

SOURCES OF
THEORY

The best way to learn theory building is to try building a theory. The motivation for your first attempt may be nothing more exciting than a class assignment. Subsequently, as you discover what theories are and how they can be used, I hope you will develop theories in order to understand something, or even just for the fun of it.

Theories are groups of ideas. We all have many ideas, and some of these are related to specific other ideas (e.g., summer, sand, and vacations; schools, children, books, teachers). We will be searching a set of sources (experience, others' reports, other theories, etc.) for three pieces of information. First, what are the concepts in a particular problem area? Second, what variables in that area are believed by any source to be important? Third, how are those ideas assumed to be related? The concepts in your problem area can come from three major sources: your own experience, the experiences of others as reported to you, and the various other social theories that have been done in the past. We will examine each source type to discover how it contributes to good theory building. The Bibliography at the end of this chapter lists examples of these various types.

EXPERIENCE

Experience can be simultaneously a help and a hindrance to good theory building. It is the richest source of motivation to *develop* theory, but it is also the most difficult source for ideas. Your own life (where you have been and what you have done, etc.) often challenges you to ask, "Why?" You are necessarily involved in yourself and your emotions. It is these involvements that give strength to motivation derived from experience. These same factors, however, also make the content of experience risky to use. Your own biases, lack of knowledge, fallibility of memory, rationalizations, repressions, inability to find or think about your subject matter, lack of mobility through time and space, poor theory, and so on are obstacles which prevent you (or any other single person) from ever knowing everything about even one single situation. These obstacles must be overcome if experience used in theory building is to differ in its truth and generality from experience used in literature. Over time, social scientists have developed techniques applicable to various obstacles which attempt both to minimize their impact and to increase the generality of theories based on experience.

Consider how you might interpret the following situations:

1. Twenty-five people are walking around in a circle in front of the city office building, blocking the entrance. The local police arrive and arrest all of the people, carrying some and leading others to waiting police vans.

2. A man carrying signs on his chest and back is passing out handbills on a street.

3. A student stands in the middle of a lecture and walks out.

Are these situations examples of "the same thing"? Before answering that question, consider that the sign carrier might be advertising and the student might have forgotten an appointment. How could you find out? Social scientists try to discipline their experiences by making explicit what they expect to find and by going beyond the simple "eyeballing" of a situation. For example, a careful study, using interviews of participants, might disclose that most of the participants in the street demonstration thought they were making a movie for an underground film maker, even though the police thought they were dealing with a real demonstration.

Even the simplest experience contains literally thousands of aspects; what you perceive depends on what strikes you and to what you compare or contrast it. If you were to observe the three situations mentioned above, you might note similarities in size, shape, clothing, speed of activity, verbalizations, race of participants, response of other persons, and so forth. These "pieces of information" would help you sort these experiences into boxes labeled "the same" or "different" and "protest" or "not."

You never experience anything without trying to fit it into preconceived categories (e.g., "civil rights demonstration," "apple," "political rally"). From science to Zen Buddhism, people agree that men have an almost incurable habit of placing all experience into little boxes which may be filed and forgotten (the boxes may be appropriate or not, the filing accurate or not). Both science and Zen Buddhism ask you to study the structure of the boxes with questioning techniques. Zen uses paradoxical questions such as: "What is the sound of one hand clapping?" Science asks a general question: "What is general, abstract, and understandable about this experience?" *General* in that the experience is not unique to one person but could, in principle, be experienced by many. *Abstract* in that some elements of the experience are selected as common characteristics of this and other experiences. *Understandable* in that people can talk about the experience.

Both Zen and science, then, are questioning the foundations of the language we use to describe our everyday experiences. And science often begins by comparing and contrasting the experience in question with other experiences which have the same name. Human memory is very fallible, particularly with respect to situations where you have been proven wrong. To help you remember what situations you have called by the same name, you might start keeping descriptions of your experiences and what resulted from them (perhaps in the format suggested on pages 18–21). You should look for situations which contrast with each other. Even in these days, however, the average American college professor and student live relatively bland, sheltered lives in which real social contrasts do not exist. If they want to use such contrasts, they must either go where things are different or use the experiences of others. And the experiences they need are those which provide contrasts between different systems of on-going activities. Contrast makes it possible to see the similarities and differences which provide bases for concept formation.

DEVELOPING CONCEPTS FROM EXPERIENCE

We can conceptualize and name appearances, actions, attitudes, outlooks, and other characteristics of persons and divide them into classes. The words which name these concepts must be clear and understandable if they are to be usable. We can all think of examples such as "fribish," which divides into "glunch," "ypistal," and "others." You should be aware that many common words make about as much understandable sense as "fribish." For example, what exactly does "intelligence," "class," or "education" mean?

To make a concept truly understandable you should use a procedure by which anyone could tell (1) whether your concept applied to a particular appearance, action, attitude, outlook, and so on, and (2) if applicable, to which class of the concept it applied. For example, any occurrence of "going to school" can be considered one class of "education." Other classes might be "informal education," "family education," and the like.

In your general observation, you should look first for experiences to which you would apply the same name and then look within these experiences for contrasts or similarities in appearance, action, attitude, outlook, and so on, and *name* these as classifications of the concept.

You can use experience as a theory source and produce general, useful concepts *if* you generalize along the lines of the following checklist:

1. What was done—name of activity? form of activity?
2. How was it done—quality of activity? process?

3. With whom?
4. With what tools or objects?
5. What initiated behavior?
6. What focus did it have—goal? person?
7. What effects did the behavior have?
8. How often did it occur and when?

Obviously, this is only a beginning, and you should also consult books which deal specifically in observation techniques (see Bibliography following this chapter).

Social scientists try to be where things are happening; they either make them happen (e.g., an experimental situation), foresee a scheduled situation (e.g., an election), or observe a natural (field) situation long enough to see things happening. In these ways they try to find (1) experiences to help them understand on-going social activity or (2) interesting questions for their general theory (motivation).

RULE 3.1 Place yourself where different or contrasting phenomena may happen in order to see similarities and differences. Verbalize or write experiences systematically to make comparisons easier. Use a checklist to insure that you include all important items.

REPORTAGE

No matter how wide ranging and systematic you are, if you limit your theoretical input to experience, your theory will be incomplete. You cannot live in the past or in two places at once. These limitations simply mean that all theorists who wish to generalize must use, either in the formulation or testing of theories, the reportage of other persons who are, or were, at a particular place when particular events occurred.

But you must be selective. You can drown in the amount of available reportage. A look at just the *New York Times Index* or the *Readers' Guide to Periodical Literature* should convince you that this statement is true. Even with careful selection there is more partial but related information, suggestive but not conclusive, on almost any conceivable topic than any one **man** can assimilate in a lifetime. Since the least search of the literature on any topic will produce numerous reports on any one item, you need to know how these reports are related. For example, might a report on the work ethic of Puritans in England be related to the occupational structure of the United States?

GENERAL DIFFICULTIES IN REPORTAGE

Care is necessary because reportage is another person's written experience, and you already know from the previous section some of the difficulties of writing down your own experiences, even for yourself alone. And it is much more difficult to write so that any possible reader could understand.

Reportage does, however, provide a range of contrasts that can motivate a theorist to ask, "Why?" It also reveals the limits of previous work. Like experience, it can provide the raw material of abstraction through contrast with other reportage and your own experience.

Reportage comes in several forms and with many distinctive problems. Some reports are systematically collected; others are not. Systematic collections may include a systematic bias; the unsystematic may be missing important elements. Some reports are written by trained observers; others are not. Social scientists, newspaper reporters, and others trained to report social events may bring to a given situation a framework of ideas which will make it impossible for them to perceive what is happening. With any reportage we must consider two contexts if we are to understand it: (1) What language is being used? (2) What is the empirical referent for a given statement (i.e., is the writer sufficiently descriptive that we can reconstruct the actual event[s])? Systematic reports by trained observers are generally characterized both by sufficient description and a consistent, if not crystal clear, language.

LANGUAGE DIFFICULTIES

Language and its usage are the most important barriers to understanding. Suppose you wanted to develop a theory about American occupational structure. You might begin with the dictionary, which provides examples of a term's use and some

range of definition with respect to words that are different
from occupation. For example:

> oc · cu · pa · tion 1a: an activity in which one engages: a
> way of passing the time <declared she had always plenty
> of ~ for herself while he was away—William Black>
> <bathing or loafing on the beaches are obviously a major
> ~ hereabouts—Ann Panners> b: the principal business
> of one's life: a craft, trade, profession or other means of
> earning a living: EMPLOYMENT, VOCATION <his ~ is farm-
> ing> <has gone from one ~ to another without settling
> down to any> <writing has been his ~ for many
> years>[1]

The dictionary provides only general meanings for a term.
A thesaurus or dictionary of synonyms provides other lists
of words and their distinctions, each word of which is very
close to the others in the set. To continue with "occupation"
we find (p. 572 of *Webster's New Dictionary of Synonyms*):
"Occupation: employment, *work, calling, pursuit, business."
The asterisk tells us that "work" is the main listing. Turning
to "work" (pp. 879–880), we find two full columns of fine
print with three major headings and half a dozen specific
terms under each, complete with examples. These listings can
be used either to group a series of classes into a higher-order
concept (e.g., trade, handicraft, art into work) or to divide a
higher-order concept into its parts (work divides into occupation, employment, calling, etc.).

As you read more sociology, the general college thesaurus
and dictionary will become less useful to you and a thesaurus/
dictionary of sociological language more important. Unfortunately, we are not currently blessed with a good thesaurus
or dictionary of social science, so you will have to write your
own as your work progresses. Several dictionaries of sociology
do exist, however, and you may find the *International Encyclopedia of the Social Sciences* (1968) useful.

[1] *Webster's 3rd New International Dictionary*, Springfield, Mass.,
G. & C. Merriam Co., 1961, p. 1560.

Now you know how "work" and "occupation" relate in standard English. You also know (if you have done some reading on this topic) that for this particular theory the Puritan work ethic of England, historically and empirically, is probably more important than that of Afghanistan to the American occupational structure. This kind of detail is necessary. If you turned to a person beside you in class and asked, "What do you mean by 'work'?" you might get a startled look and then perhaps a philosophical discussion of "labor." Shortly, neither of you would be able to use the word freely because it would mean so much that it would seem wrong to use it at all.

You should note that, until you are challenged, you can and do use very difficult concepts often and with ease. Concepts like "love," "law," and "peace" are part of the vocabulary you use. A challenge regarding their meaning would probably seem an unnecessary wrangle about words. But if you want others to know precisely what you mean, then you must wrangle now to avoid misunderstandings later.

Often such wrangles can be resolved by saying: "That's what I mean," as you point to an aardvark or heliotrope or other physically present item. Pointing to attributes and abstractions, however, is more difficult (pointing to an attribute requires that you say something like, "Look at the following nineteen things. What I mean is what is common about them.").

When analyzing a social institution, you will rarely be discussing a physically present item. Almost always you will be concerned with an attribute of a situation, person, group, or thing. As you can see if you think about it, there are many more attributes than things. One rock has weight, size, color, hardness, reflectivity, and so on. One social situation has, among other attributes which could be considered, the emotions of its respondents, their physical location and movements, speeches if any, and appearance. One or even several examples do not make it immediately obvious to an outsider which attribute of a situation is under study, so you must specify as well as have examples.

Definitional problems persist only when you insist that another person understand what you are doing or saying. Each person may and probably does have a private language which no one else completely understands. He may thereby define any combination of sounds, letters, or other symbols to mean (signify) anything he wants. But theory is a fundamentally social language; private meanings cannot be permitted. Therefore, some means for systematically assuring that one word or symbol has the same meaning for all parties must be found. The abstractions implicit in theory require even greater clarity than ordinary language and must be given procedures whereby anyone, whether the investigator's maiden aunt or an Indonesian sociologist, can understand perfectly whether or not he or she is looking at a concrete example of the abstraction. These procedures are sometimes called operations (particularly when the procedure is mechanical as is often true in physical theory). Communication is based upon agreement by those concerned on the code and content of a message. You must pay a price if you change that code: others may not understand you (lack of communication), and they may resent the liberties you have taken.

Communication is difficult because most English words have several meanings depending on context. In order to specify what you mean, you must define all major terms. For example, in the United States, in general, college is an educational institution which provides at least the 13th and 14th years of formal education. By "college" do you mean to include or exclude graduate schools? Contrast several cases to bring out attributes. College also relates to terms such as "education," "post-high school," and "professor." The set of terms that you choose should be those commonly used by the group that you expect to understand what you are saying. Examples of such groups are: professional sociologists, college students at "X" college, taxi drivers.

Definitions are intended as aids to understanding, and they should be written as such. The risk involved in theory building becomes clearer when we realize that, for much of our ordinary conversation, no one cares what is being said. Often the point of an argument is to "close out" one's opponent, leaving him nothing further to say. We often do this with rhetorical gimmicks and verbal obfuscation. By contrast a theory should make disproof very easy by being very clear.

To summarize the above discussion:

RULE 3.2   Use simple procedures to define terms empirically.

RULE 3.3   Decide which group you are writing for; then select an appropriate set of terms from the language of that group.

EMPIRICAL ASPECTS

Reportage also has an empirical aspect. If a child comes to you and says, "Johnny hit me," you have at least two possible responses: "It it true?" and "Why?" "Why" is the theorist's response; "Is it true?" is the data gatherer's. Both of these approaches are necessary for good research, but while you are studying theory, you should accept as valid all available data until given good reason to decide that some is unacceptable. You will want to list your data sources and note your judgment (highly reliable, hearsay, etc.) of their accuracy. At first you may only be able to note whether or not a report strikes you as competent. Later, as you gain more methodological skill and broader understanding of the errors which reports can contain, you can be more specific with respect to strengths and weaknesses.

You may better understand empirical reports if you (roughly) graph the values of a few variables against one another or against time. For example, you might want to graph the number of training years required to practice certain professions against the pay in those professions. To do this use graph paper (or draw your own lines on regular paper); let each bottom line represent one year of training and each side line $200. Don't worry too much about the accuracy of your divisions; if you make an error, you can always change or redraw the graph.

Then as you read, for example, about doctors, you may find that training takes ten years and starting salaries average $10,000; a computer specialist trains about two years and starts at roughly $14,000. Other professions will provide several more points for your graph. These points form a scatter-plot. The Bibliography following this chapter lists several very good sources to help you interpret these simple graphs. For now, however, you are simply collecting information. Always list your data sources on either the front or the back of your charts so that two months later, when you reexamine them, you will not find it necessary to search for the data sources again.

RULE 3.4   Believe data until you are given good reason to dis-believe it. Graph empirical values as you collect them to help you understand what is happening.

OTHER
SOCIAL THEORIES

Social theories other than your own are not always clearly identified as such. Much reportage contains implicit theories as well as the empirical facts of a case. Indeed, a major difficulty in using reportage is separating theory from data. Besides reportage, other theories also contain philosophy, social problem statements, and empirical or quasi-empirical reports. You need to separate these aspects of other theories from one another and use them appropriately.

PHILOSOPHY

Certain fundamental issues relate to how man views his world. Reflection on these issues (which have plagued thinkers for years) has produced statements like "Democracy is a fraud" or "Men are governed by self-interest." These statements are not intended as parts of an empirically oriented theory but rather as suggestions about what kinds of things relate to other kinds of things. For example, "fraud" relates to "democracy," "self-interest" to "men"; if we believe the statements above, they then provide a set of relations for words.

Philosophy in its pure form can (1) add concepts to a net of relations (metaphysics), (2) give rules for the manipulation of relations in that net (logic), and (3) evaluate critically other nets of relations that nonphilosophers (e.g., theologians, scientists, and "the man in the street") have created to provide order to their ideas. As such, philosophy can help us discern when our ideas are inconsistent or when we are manipulating inappropriately.

But philosophical ideas have no empirical component and are not subject to test against reality. They are not, then, theories and, while they can provide structure for theories, we must go beyond them by adding relevant empirical referents to our ideas.

RULE 3.5   Philosophy can provide (1) concepts, (2) rules for the manipulation of relations, and (3) evaluation for nets of relations. Relevant empirical references are necessary if philosophical statements are to become parts of a theory.

SOCIAL PROBLEM STATEMENTS

Whenever decisions about a social process or activity must be made, the theorist is faced with difficulties created because (1) the decision will directly affect his actions or someone else's (when possible, a theorist should attempt to analyze his own personal actions; we will consider procedures for doing this in Chapters 8, 9, and 10). (2) The theorist empathizes with those who are powerless and distrusts those who are powerful (or vice versa). The difficulty here is for the theorist to keep his own feelings from so distorting his thinking that neither he nor anyone else can trust his theory to be true or even close to truth. (3) The decisions suggested by theory produce inconsistent positions or actions. Such situations can be creative focuses for research and act as motivators for theory.

Involvement, empathy, and inconsistent results can all provide powerful motivation to develop a theory and subsequently to act from that theory. They may also provide content areas for theory. Research reports on these problems, however, must respond to questions raised by all sides of an issue if they are to be significant. It is not good for a theorist's analytical ability to do research for one party to a dispute simply because that party wants it done. If you are working on a contentious problem, you should seek critical aid from as many other theorists as are readily available. If such aid is lacking, you are likely to produce very personal or very biased theory incorporating a very high probability of error.

RULE 3.6   Social problems can motivate and focus research; as a novice, move into a social problem area carefully.

EMPIRICAL AND QUASI-EMPIRICAL REPORTS

Someone, somewhere, sometime, has done empirical research on almost every conceivable topic. Much of this research is useless because it is confused, inaccurate, biased, unclear, or false. Your own personal theories may fall into this category. When working with such material, your task is to add accurate material when you can, remove erroneous parts, and bring sense out of the remainder.

Many empirical generalizations found in social science literature are stated as a simple relation between two variables. Prototype statements are: (1) the greater the X, the greater the Y; and more commonly, (2) A's tend to be associated with B's. These statements may or may not be testable depending on the measures available. You may not be able to determine the accuracy of observations or the reliability of generalizations at this point. While you are still learning the basics of theory building, simply accept the data given you.

Books are not the only data source for propositions. You might also use:

1. Data collected by government agencies for general purposes (e.g., population census, statistical abstract materials);
2. Old polls (Roper Center, National Opinion Research Center, etc.);
3. Data on processes (freight car movements, etc.);
4. Research reports about the place, time, or group of interest;
5. Any available newspaper, magazine, etc., material.

You must read widely in any area that you intend to study seriously. This job unfortunately cannot be routinized and given to a computer because neither a computer nor a statistician can tell you whether a given statement will ultimately prove to be interesting.

In examining the data in any report you should:

1. Look for regularities.
2. Look for big differences; those that require detailed analysis are not generally too useful during the initial stage of theory building.
3. Look for patterns. Graphs and charts of the data will help you see these patterns.
4. Hold out some data as a check against the apparent regularities that small samples give. If you are short of data (e.g., there are only so many business cycles, elections, civil wars), you still should hold out one (perhaps the last) as a check against the rest.

When you finish a particular book, article, or other source, you should summarize your impression of that piece of research. The following checklist may help:

1. What questions is the author intending to answer?
   a) Do they relate to your questions? (If not, you are probably wasting time reading him.)
   b) Do they relate to the questions of others you are reading? If not, is his approach different enough to suggest helpful contrasts?
2. How does he use data?
   a) How good are the data? Does he have:
      (1) reasonable sampling,
      (2) measurement validity,
      (3) controls or checks on collection?
   b) Does it affect his conclusions and the rest of his discussion, or are his conclusions really independent of his data?
3. What is the structure of his theory?
   a) Are his assumptions, measures, variables, concepts, and relations among concepts clearly stated?
   b) Are his concepts systematically related, not contradictory, and appropriate?

    c) Is the theory in the form of:
       (1) a cause-and-effect listing?
       (2) a propositional inventory?
       (3) a discourse with some data?
       (4) other?

After reading one or two pieces, you will want to know whether there are more that would be useful later. There are several ways to find such a set of helpful readings:

1. Ask someone who might know, for example, an instructor or person doing research in the area.
2. Use reading lists from appropriate courses.
3. Tell people what you are doing and listen for suggestions.
4. Use a library's subject listings and reference facilities; browsing through appropriate sections of the stacks can be especially helpful.
5. Use abstracting services. *Sociological Abstracts* and the *International Social Science Abstracts* are both good sources.
6. Use the good propositional inventories available in several areas, for example, Anthony Downs' *Inside Bureaucracy*. (This and other propositional inventories are noted in the Bibliography at the end of this chapter.) These can help you shortcut both reference work and systematization.

When you have reached the end of your initial resources, it is time to begin thinking about the results. For example, if you continued developing the theory about American occupational structure begun above, you might know from observation that the data seem to lump specific kinds of occupations together. From a theory of occupational mobility you may know that physical and social mobility should be distinguished, although you are not certain in practice what either means. From reportage you may have some idea of the range of human activities that have been considered occupations at some time and place and of the differences that often exist between job descriptions and the actual performance of duties. Ordering this information is your next task.

SUMMARY

We have considered three major sources of theories: personal experience, the reports of others, and other social theories. Each has its difficulties and strengths as a source for general, abstract, understandable social theory. Each can produce content for theories and motivation for further work.

The first step in theory building concerns your sources. Consider your own experience and write out some conclusions. Look at reports that you or someone else believes might be helpful. Then search for applicable, relevant theories which provide some systematic raw material for your theory. When you are through, you will have an untidy pile of information. This will be the basic source of material with which you continue.

One note on systematization. You should expect, as you systematically build a theory, to find that you have not collected quite the right material or that something very essential is missing. There is no correct amount of material that you must collect, nor, if you are careful, is there an end to the "relevant" information you might collect. You will probably need to return to the sources of your theory for more information, ideas, or inspiration. This necessity should not be discouraging; in fact, it should cause you to begin the building process as soon as possible so that your work will be as accurate and complete as possible.

RULES

RULE 3.1   Place yourself where different or contrasting phenomena may happen in order to see similarities and differences. Verbalize or write experiences systematically to make comparisons easier. Use a checklist to insure that you include all important items.

RULE 3.2   Use simple procedures to define terms empirically.

RULE 3.3   Decide which group you are writing for; then select an appropriate set of terms from the language of that group.

RULE 3.4   Believe data until you are given good reason to disbelieve it. Graph empirical values as you collect them to help you understand what is happening.

RULE 3.5   Philosophy can provide (1) concepts, (2) rules for the manipulation of relations, and (3) evaluation for nets of relations. Relevant empirical references are necessary if philosophical statements are to become parts of a theory.

RULE 3.6   Social problems can motivate and focus research; as a novice, move into a social problem area carefully.

EXERCISE

1. Start collecting information from several different sources on a problem that interests you. List relevant concepts, variables, and relations.

BIBLIOGRAPHY

CLARK, KENNETH B., and JEANNETTE HOPKINS. *A Relevant War Against Poverty: A Study of Community Action Programs and Observable Social Change.* New York: Harper & Row, 1970.

   A statement of a social problem and an empirical report evaluating a public program.

DOWNS, ANTHONY. *Inside Bureaucracy.* Boston: Little, Brown and Company, 1967.

   A propositional inventory with a great deal of explanation about organization.

GEERTZ, CLIFFORD. *The Religion of Java.* New York: The Free Press, 1964.

   An empirical report.

GORDEN, RAYMOND L. *Interviewing: Strategy, Techniques and Tactics.* Homewood, Ill.: The Dorsey Press, 1969.

   A thorough review of interviewing techniques which can help you to systematize experience.

KELLER, SUZANNE. *Beyond the Ruling Class: Strategic Elites in Modern Society.* New York: Random House, 1963.

A quasi-empirical report summarizing other material.

LEWIS, OSCAR. *Five Families: Mexican Case Studies in the Culture of Poverty.* New York: Mentor Books, 1959.

Most of this book is reportage with some attempt at systematization.

LIEBOW, ELLIOT. *Tally's Corner.* Boston: Little, Brown and Company, 1967.

A statement of a social problem.

MARCH, JAMES G., and HERBERT A. SIMON. *Organizations.* New York: John Wiley & Sons, Inc., 1958.

Another propositional inventory on organizations.

MARCUSE, HERBERT. *Eros and Civilization: A Philosophical Inquiry into Freud.* New York: Vintage Books, 1962.

An example of philosophical work.

MYRDAL, JAN. *Report from a Chinese Village.* New York: Signet Books, 1965.

Like Lewis, Myrdal is primarily a reporter of a particular setting.

PARSONS, TALCOTT. *Societies: Evolutionary and Comparative Perspectives.* Englewood Cliffs, N.J.: Prentice-Hall, Inc., 1966.

An example of development of a conceptual system which I have called "philosophy."

SOLZHENITSYN, ALEXSANDR L. *The First Circle.* New York: Bantam Books, 1969.

Fiction can also be good reportage. Realistic novels and short stories are particularly good. This is an excellent example.

Chapter 4

THEORY
CONNECTIONS

Theories bridge the gap between language and experience using the concept-variable units described in Chapter 2. In this chapter I will discuss the connection of concept-variable units as well as the problems which accompany this step in theory building.

In general, single statements relating two concepts (e.g., crisis situations decrease decentralization) are either true or false or possibly just misleading, but they are rarely very interesting. They offer a guide for those interested in just those two concepts, but they provide no intellectual structure; even thousands of such statements do not necessarily constitute an interesting theory.

Such statements can be important, however, as the *building blocks* of theory. We can combine statements either by:

1. Connecting more than two concepts with relations, or
2. Joining concepts into higher-order concepts.

CONNECTING CONCEPTS
WITH RELATIONS

When I discussed relations in Chapter 2 (pp. 23–25), I indicated how two concepts might be connected by a relation. For example, in examining "decentralization" and "similarity"

(Berelson and Steiner, A4), I noted that one could produce changes in similarity with changes in decentralization and not vice versa; thus Rule 2.8*a* would apply. On that basis I assigned direction to the asymmetry and, having defined the two concepts as I did, could further determine that they were negatively related. That relation was drawn as:

decentralization $---\rightarrow$ similarity

Looking further through the concepts defined in Chapter 2, I find "crisis." If we consider statement A4.2, we note that Berelson and Steiner, following several other authors, suggest that times of crisis lead to centralization. If, as is likely, Rule 2.8*b* applies, we have an asymmetric relation between "crisis" and "decentralization" that is also negative. It, too, can be drawn:

crisis $---\rightarrow$ decentralization

Now, with these two statements, can we state a relation between "crisis" and "similarity" even if, as is the case, Berelson and Steiner say nothing about such a relation?

TRANSITIVITY: STATISTICAL AND DETERMINISTIC RELATIONS

Before making any such statement, we must decide which properties of the relations in our theory will be *transitive*. Transitivity of relations operates as follows: if A is related to B, and B is related to C, then A will relate to C as it does to B, given that the relation is transitive. We noted three properties of relations in Chapter 2: association, sign, and asymmetry. For any particular theory we are building, we must decide which of these properties, for any pair of concepts, is transitive. For the purposes of this book we will consider two kinds of theory relations: (1) *statistical*, in which association and sign are transitive; (2) *deterministic* (used exclusively in Chapters 4–7) in which *all* properties of the relation are transitive.[1]

---

[1] Decisions about transitivity must ultimately be made by the theorist, taking into account (1) the expressed statements of his sources and (2) the kind of theory he wants to build. Deterministic theories contain more implications and so are richer, more interesting and more valuable. They are also more likely to be wrong or inconsistent when tested against actual data.

The kind of relation asserted becomes important when we examine the *implications* of a theory's original assertions. For instance, in the "crisis," "decentralization," and "similarity" example, "crisis" was negatively related to "decentralization," and "decentralization" negatively related to "similarity." Figure 4.1*a* shows this diagrammatically. If this theory has only statistical relations, we will show the relation between "crisis" and "similarity" as a positive, signed association with no direction (see Figure 4.1*b*). If deterministic relations hold for this theory, however, we can show a positive association from "crisis" to "similarity" (see Figure 4.1*c*) as an *implication*.

Figure 4.1 Simple Implications of Statistical and Deterministic Relations

a. Original assertions:

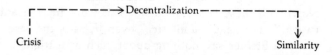

b. Implication: statistical relations

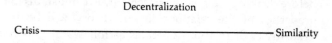

c. Implication: deterministic relations

Decentralization

Crisis ————————————————————→ Similarity

The differences between deterministic and statistical theories become more apparent as more concepts are added. Let's take Berelson and Steiner's final assertion in A4, that "decentralization" is positively related to "tolerance." I then add (from G. Homans, 1950) that "similarity" is positively related to "liking" and (from my own thinking) that "tolerance" relates positively to "communication." We now have a group of assertions which can be diagrammed as in Figure 4.2*a*.

Figure 4.2*b* shows the implications of the assertions in 4.2*a* if the theory is statistical. There are four implications, none of which has more than one intermediate concept. Figure 4.2*c* shows the implications if the theory is deterministic. (For purposes of this book, in further consideration of the Berel-

Figure 4.2 Complex Implications of Statistical and Deterministic Relations

a. Assertions

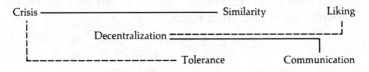

b. Implications: statistical theory

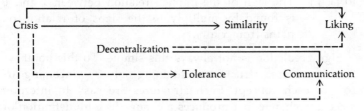

c. Implications: deterministic theory

d. Implications: no association
Similarity-tolerance   Similarity-communication
Tolerance-liking   Liking-communication

son and Steiner material, I will assume a deterministic theory.) There are six implications, none of which is limited to one intermediate concept; like the "crisis"-"liking" relation, each relation can have many intermediates. Figure 4.2*d* lists those concept pairs which show *no* relation in the theory, either stated or implied. (It is important to know relations as well as non-relations when you begin testing a theory.)

SIGN RULE

The sign of the implied relation between two concepts in a deterministic theory composed of signed relations can be computed as follows:

1. Take all paths leading from one concept to a second, following the arrows.

2a. If no path exists, you can make *no* prediction.

2b. If one path exists, multiply the signs of the relations by each other.

2c. If two or more paths exist between the same two concepts, multiply the signs along each path and determine whether they agree. If they do, accept the sign. If not, the theory has inconsistent predictions. Two consistent theories should then be developed and tested against each other. For example, we predict from Figure 4.2a that

$$\text{crisis} \longrightarrow \text{liking}$$
$$\text{crisis} \longrightarrow \text{similarity}$$
$$\text{decentralization} - - - - \to \text{liking}$$

RULE 4.1 The sign of the implied relation between x and y is found by multiplying the signs of relation on paths from x to y.

Sign prediction is not always this simple. To this point we have considered structures containing only *one* incoming arrow to each concept. Such structures are easy to interpret since any change in x produces a change in y by definition of the relation. Two other, more complex, structures exist in which *more* than one arrow comes to a concept from other concepts.

The first of these represents an *"or"* situation. Statement A4 of the Berelson and Steiner material provides an example of this situation, asserting that more "channels of communication" are associated with less "similarity"; we thus have a negative relation between "channel" and "similarity" to add to Figure 4.2a. The result is shown in Figure 4.3. Now note that "decentralization" already shows a negative relation to "similarity." Thus either "channels" *or* "decentralization" can lessen "similarity." In interpreting these two arrows,

Figure 4.3 Berelson and Steiner Theory of Organization: Part 1

"Channel" $------\rightarrow$ Similarity
$\uparrow$
$\vert$
$\vert$
$\vert$
Crisis $----------\rightarrow$ Decentralization

we must know whether both of the preceding concepts ("channels" and "decentralization") imply the same sign for "similarity." If they do, the interpretation is clear; "similarity" is simply given that sign. When two *different* implications are made, however (e.g., "decentralization" implies positive and "channels," negative), we can draw no implication as long as the concepts are dichotomous relations of equal strength; either concept is equally likely to produce an effect. Table 4.1 shows all possible outcomes for "similarity" given

Table 4.1 Example of *Or:* The Sign of "Similarity"

		decentralization	
		−	+
channel	+	?	−
	−	+	?

an *or* relation. If your theory contains this structure, you may want to use the algebraic treatment discussed in Chapter 7 (pp. 113–117).

Statement A4.1 demonstrates the second complex structure. The statement is made that both "decentralization" *and* "visibility" are necessary before "identification" will occur (see Figure 4.4). The mechanics of sign prediction for *and*

Figure 4.4 Berelson and Steiner Theory of Organization: Part 2

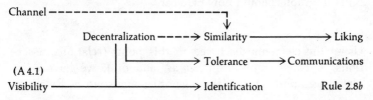

Channel $---------------------$
$\downarrow$
Decentralization $----\rightarrow$ Similarity $\longrightarrow$ Liking
$\longrightarrow$ Tolerance $\longrightarrow$ Communications
(A 4.1)
Visibility $\longrightarrow$ Identification   Rule 2.8*b*

relations operate similarly to *or* situations except that the resolution with inconsistent predictions is different. Instead of asserting an indeterminant relation, we assert *no* relation when the prior concepts lack identical implications. Table 4.2

Table 4.2 Example of *And:* The Sign of "Identification"

	decentralization	
	−	+
visibility +	0	+
−	−	0

shows all possible outcomes for "identification," given an *and* relation. When you draw an *and* relation, represent the *and* by joining the arrows from the preceding concepts *before* they reach the succeeding concept (e.g., "identification"). (Note the difference between Figures 4.3 and 4.4 in this respect.)

Let us add to the material in Figure 4.2 one final concept from my own thinking: "identification" leads to "support" (see Figure 4.5). The sign is simple to predict, with no *ands*

Figure 4.5 Complete Berelson and Steiner Theory of Organization

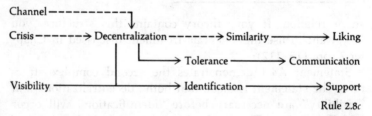

Rule 2.8c

or *ors* involved. The graph now has 10 concepts connected by 8 relations. It is not finished, but the process of relating concepts in graphs should now be clear.

SUMMARY

Using the elements discussed to this point (relations, assertions, signs of implications, *ands*, and *ors*), we have completed a graph from the language of several sources. Relations are linkages between concepts. They connect groups of concepts into graphs which subsequently provide a basis for empirical and logical analysis. The difference between these groups of associated concepts that we are calling social theory and other connected groups (e.g., concepts in much of philosophy) is that empirical references exist for many of the theory's terms, and thus a language's aptness at description or explanation can be either demonstrated or shown to be lacking.

RULE 4.2 *a*) Concepts may be linked by relations into sets of concepts. These sets may be diagrammed as graphs.

b) The assertions of a theory will produce implications through applications of the sign rule and the asymmetries of deterministic theory.

RULE 4.3 As a beginning theorist, assume determinism in your theories.

BEGINNINGS AND ENDINGS FOR THEORY STRUCTURE

After you have joined your concepts, lay them out on paper so that as many as possible of the asymmetry arrows move from left to right (see Figure 4.5). This device facilitates clear thinking and will help you to locate the beginning(s) and ending(s) of your theory.

When concepts are related asymmetrically (i.e., have directed relationships), it is possible to have one or more concepts that relate only *to* other concepts and one or more that only *receive* a relationship *from* other concepts. For any particular theory, if a concept (or concepts) has relationships leading only *from* it, it is the *beginning* of the theory. If there is a concept (or concepts) to which relations only *come*, that is the *ending* of the theory.

The set of beginnings for a given theory is that set of concepts whose interconnections are not important, at least for the purposes of that theory. It is not true that nothing "caused" these concepts; we have simply made a provisional decision not to find *their* beginnings. Beginning concepts are a psychologically acceptable starting place for an investigator, often because his competence ends there. For sociology, concepts such as "age" and "sex" often constitute beginning concepts for theory because sociologists are not prepared to analyze the genetics and demography that produce a certain age-sex ratio.

The endings for a theory are those things that a theory is intended to explain. As with beginnings, a concept's status as an ending does not indicate that it has no effects; it is simply an arbitrary stopping place for the theory-building process. For sociology, the stopping points of theory are often such ideas as "bureaucracy," "social control," and the like. Investigators frequently begin with a concept that they want to explain and then move backward through the literature, finding things that are assumed to "cause" that particular concept.

RULE 4.4   Designate what you want explained as the ending of your theory and then look for its causes (and the causes of those causes, etc.) until you exhaust the literature you are searching.

EXAMPLE. In Figure 4.5, "channel," "crisis," and "visibility" are beginnings; "liking," "communication," and "support" are endings.

CONNECTEDNESS

Two concepts are connected if there is a relation or a series of relations between them. We can distinguish (1) *simple* connectedness, in which we disregard the direction of asymmetries and only require that *some* set of relations form a path between the two, from (2) *direct* connectedness, in which the *order* of the concepts and the *direction* of the arrows are important. For example, all of the concepts in Figure 4.5 are simply connected to one another and to nothing else. "Channel" is *directly* connected to "liking" but not to "decentralization" or "support." "Liking" is not directly connected to any other concept. In deterministic theory implications result from direct connectedness between pairs of concepts.

When we describe a graph of concepts, we can measure (1) density and (2) direct connectedness. *Density* is the number of assertions made by a theory as a percentage of the number of possible assertions. Count one actual assertion for each pair of concepts simply connected by a relation. The number of *possible* assertions is: the number (N) of concepts times the number of concepts minus one, or $N(N-1)$. (Table 4.3 shows the number of possible relations for certain numbers of concepts.) Figure 4.5 shows 10 concepts. The number of possible assertions is 10(9) or 90, and of actual assertions, 9. The graph is thus 10 percent dense.

Table 4.3 Number of Possible Relations
$[N(N-1)]$ for Various Numbers of Concepts

Concepts	Possible Asymmetric Relations
N	$N(N-1)$
2	2
3	6
4	12
5	20
6	30
7	42
8	56
9	72
10	90
11	110
12	132
20	380
30	870
40	1560
50	2450

Direct connectedness is the total number of assertions *plus* implications made by a theory as a percentage of the number of possible assertions. In Figure 4.5 there are 16 assertions plus implications; the graph is 18 percent directly connected.

As a system's density increases, its direct connectedness normally increases. At some point it will become impossible to change anything because relations among earlier concepts will have determined the sign and value of later parts of the system. Testing the whole system becomes easier, however, because any set of concepts will have impact on the whole theoretical system.

The relation between connectedness and density is rather complex. A good theory is precisely as connected as necessary to include all that is known and to order that knowledge, but it should simultaneously have a low density. To state this differently, good theory should have a few well-chosen, originally stated relations (low density) whose implications are all that is known or believed about a topic (high connectedness). For example, in Figure 4.5 the original density was 10 percent; the addition of six implications made the theory 18 percent connected. This 18 percent does not constitute particularly high connectedness, but it may be sufficient. In Chapter 6 I will consider how a theory may be overconnected.

You should note the existence and significance of minimum densities. Less than $N - 1$ connections among N concepts leaves some concepts (or sets of concepts) not simply connected. If you have a concept that is not simply connected to others in the theory, either connect it or treat the separate parts as separate theory alternatives. A theory must achieve minimum density before it can be treated as a theory.

RULE 4.5   *a*) After graphing a theory and locating its beginnings and endings, compute its density and connectedness.

          b) A good theory has low density and high connectedness.

RULE 4.6   If your theory is not simply connected, either connect it or treat each simply connected part separately.

CYCLES

A cycle occurs when a concept links to other concepts in such a manner that it becomes its own cause. For example (Figure 4.5), if "support" caused "crisis," we would find a direct connection between "support" and "support." We have not considered cycles, and I suggest you avoid them because they require advanced techniques for testing and interpretation. If your theory produces a cycle, break it at some point and consider it a timebound (see below, pp. 67–68) segment of the total process.

RULE 4.7 Avoid cycles in simple theories. Eliminate them if you have them.

SUMMARY

To begin building a theory by connecting concepts with relations: (1) start with the relations you have collected (as in Chapter 2); (2) graph all the relations, connecting two or more concepts as the assertions state; (3) rearrange the graph with beginnings on the left, endings on the right, and as many arrows as possible moving from left to right; (4) check for simple connectedness (if each concept in your structure is not simply connected to each other concept, either connect the loose concepts or treat each part separately); (5) calculate density and direct connectedness. Is the density low and the connectedness high? If not, are some assertions unnecessary because their connections are also included as implications and they add no new implications?

It is possible to go wild with causal models and produce a "grand causal model" containing all of the concepts that have ever occurred to anyone. It is quite impractical to do so, however. First, you would have too many propositions to test or to use in any other way. Further, it is characteristic of the social sciences that firm propositions are scattered rather than dense, and thus it is empirically most unlikely that you could produce a "grand causal model" for the social sciences.

Your goal is to produce theories with a high level of generality that still contain enough specifics to generate a sophisticated and complete theory in a particular area. You will probably do a little "blue skying" in order to join your concepts initially. After that, however, you should tie your relations firmly to reality and evaluate the truth of the many alternate models you have proposed.

HIGHER-ORDER
CONCEPTS

Concepts can be assigned to higher-order concepts composed of other concepts. As we noted in Chapter 3, a concept is composed of subconcepts, each of which is directly linked to some class or classes of a variable. The concept itself is linked to the whole variable and thus is very close to being empirically definable itself. A higher-order concept is created by linking at least two "empirical" concepts and defining their conjunction (see Figure 4.6). For example, "crisis" in an or-

Figure 4.6 The Reduction of Experiences into Higher-Order Concepts

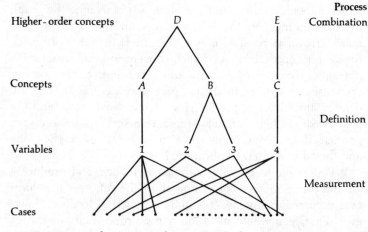

ganization produces "similarity," a lack of "tolerance," and low "identification" with the organization. An organization lacking "crisis" has "tolerance," "diversity," and high "identification." We might want to conceptualize these two distinctions as "crisis organization" and "noncrisis organization." Other items could then be related to these two higher-order concepts.

For example, in a "crisis organization" people like one another, communicate with one another, and, if they know one another, support one another. This statement simply summarizes the theory graphed in Figure 4.5, but the higher-order concept helps to clarify it.

Social scientists are strongly inclined to overuse higher-order concepts and to define ideas rather than use them in theories. Definition in *combination* with relational theory, however, can produce a very strong result. I stated earlier that, for the beginning theorist, one level of concepts and one level of subconcepts should be sufficient. This should prevent him from developing what I call the *elaboration game*, that is, the piling of concept on higher-order concept, not to gain clarity but to make the theory sound more adequate by making it more complex. This game perverts the purpose of social science, which is to develop intellectual models and describe and explain data. The line between theoretical adequacy, through elaboration, and the elaboration game is so thin that beginning theorists should adhere strictly to two levels (concept and subconcept) until they understand more fully how empirical testing works and what theory structure implies for that testing.

TIME IN
RELATIONS

As you diagram your theory, you will probably find several questions not directly answered by the diagram:

1. Does the effect happen quickly or is there a lengthy delay?
2. Is there any indication that the prediction is complex in form (nonlinearity, etc.)?[2]

The first question considers duration of time. You can build either timeless or timebound models. A timeless one expects events either to happen instantaneously or to be already completed so that no time lag exists. For example, if we observe two people talking and responding to each other, we can state a rather unexciting proposition: Talking by one of two persons in a party tends to produce talking by the other. This model is timeless in that the response is quick enough to be considered instantaneous. If we examine, in an adult population, "father's education" and "son's education"

[2] Paraphrased from H. Blalock (1969).

as two related concepts, we might put them in a timeless relation as well because the direct effects of a father's education on the son's ought to be completed by the time the son is an adult.

Timebound models can include either a specific date or upper and lower time limits dependent on other factors. Take the statement, "Certain kinds of legislation will not be passed by Congress during this administration's tenure even if they were likely on the basis of other factors." A model based on this statement will depend on specific dates. You might, therefore, suggest the following: "Legislation will pass in 1973 or 1977, depending on which date sees the passing of the present administration." If, to take a different problem, you know in detail the time that certain activities take, you may state a minimum time. If you wanted to rebuild New York City, for example, you might state that the job would take three years if you had unlimited funds and cooperation. Using detailed information, we often can set upper and lower time limits (e.g., the New York rebuilding job will take three $+ x$ years, given specific limits on funds and cooperation).

Early in this chapter I noted two different kinds of relationships, statistical and deterministic. These respond differently to time. In statistical relationships a second variable *tends* to follow the first, or the two *tend* to be associated. With these relationships there is a finite probability that a prediction will be wrong. Many of the empirical relationships reported in the literature you are reading (and from which you may wish to generalize) are statistical in nature.

In a deterministic relationship, one variable takes a value and the second variable will respond predictably, depending on sign and time constraints. Causal relations are usually seen as deterministic with additional concepts brought in to explain any variance from prediction.

A brief word about complex relationships is in order. The foregoing discussion has assumed that, within a theory, two variables are simply related; if related positively, they relate positively and to the same degree over the whole range of values in which they occur. Obviously relationships exist in which these conditions do not hold. The law of diminishing returns provides such an example: If you produce more, in general you sell more until you begin to satisfy the market for your product, and then you slowly start to sell less. Such behavior produces a curvilinear relationship between production and sales. Other complexities could be cited. For this text we will continue to assume a simple linear model without complex relationships since the basic techniques with which we are immediately concerned do not hold for complex situations.[3] As you progress beyond introductory theory, you will learn techniques for handling more complex relationships.

RULE 4.8   As a beginning theorist, assume simple linear relations for all your models.

RULES

RULE 4.1   The sign of the implied relation between x and y is found by multiplying the signs of relations on paths from x to y.

RULE 4.2   *a*) Concepts may be linked by relations into sets of concepts. These sets may be diagrammed as graphs.

   b) The assertions of a theory will produce implications through applications of the sign rule and the asymmetries of deterministic theory.

RULE 4.3   As a beginning theorist, assume determinism in your theories.

RULE 4.4   Designate what you want explained as the ending of your theory and then look for its causes (and the causes of those causes, etc.) until you exhaust the literature you are searching.

---

[3] Linearity is not a severe restriction. We can later transform variables to make their relations linear, or nonlinear effects may be linear in their range of interest. This whole topic is well discussed in W. H. Huggins and D. Entwisle (1969).

RULE 4.5 *a*) After graphing a theory and locating its beginnings and endings, compute its density and
connectedness.

b) A good theory has low density and high connectedness.

RULE 4.6 If your theory is not simply connected, either connect it or treat each simply connected part separately.

RULE 4.7 Avoid cycles in simple theories. Eliminate them if
you have them.

RULE 4.8 As a beginning theorist, assume simple linear relations for all your models.

EXERCISES

1. Continue diagramming the Berelson and Steiner material
   from propositions A5 and A6 as an exercise. (Note: You
   may not emerge with a simply connected diagram.)
2. Take at least five concepts (maximum twenty) from some
   written work and put them into dichotomous form. Find
   relations among these five that are explicitly stated (give
   references). You will need at least four. If you cannot find
   four, make up the rest and indicate that you have done so.
   a) State each relation.
   b) State the rule under which it is a relation.
   c) Involve each of your five concepts at least once in a
       relation.
   d) Graph the theory using these relations.
   e) Following the Summary on p. 65, complete graphing
       this theory.
3. *a*) Change one premise to its opposite and repeat the exer-
       cise. (Instead of "X is positively related to Y," use "X
       is negatively related to Y.") What differences occur in
       implications? Why?
   b) Change another premise and restore the first. Are there
       any differences in the changes? What are they?

c) Change the first premise to its complement (change "*X* is positively related to *Y*" to "*Y* is positively related to *X*"). What differences does this make? Why?

BIBLIOGRAPHY

BLALOCK, HUBERT. *Theory Construction*. Englewood Cliffs, N.J.: Prentice-Hall, 1969.

Chapters 1 through 3 detail a similar process of theory construction.

HUGGINS, W. H., and DORIS R. ENTWISLE. *Introductory Systems and Design*. Waltham, Mass.: Blaisdell Publishing Co., 1968.

A well-organized and self-instructing introduction to the problems and power of operator graphs as a symbolization for linear systems.

STINCHCOMBE, ARTHUR. *Constructing Social Theories*. New York: Harcourt Brace Jovanovich, 1968.

Uses similar concept-relation models. Requires some knowledge of sociology to understand.

Chapter 5

EMPIRICAL DECISIONS
ABOUT THEORY

Concepts, relations, definitions, and variables are the formal machinery of theory building. In this chapter we will discuss the empirical decisions you must make about that formal machinery using measurement, functions, and a standard for determining whether your functions support your relations. *Measurement* reports empirical reality in terms of the variables you have established. *Functions* describe the content that measurement puts into a variable and how this content resembles or differs from that put into one or several other variables. The *standard* tests whether the function between two variables is that predicted by the relation among their associated concepts.

A major criterion for good theory is how well it orders data into sensible intellectual patterns. We must do more than make theory empirically meaningful; we must also make the myriad results of empirical research (i.e., sampling, measuring, tabulating, calculating, interpreting, etc.) meaningful in theoretical terms. We can show that some prototheories do not fit the data very well and that we have no prototheories for some data.

MEASUREMENT
Social information is measured through responses to tests and questionnaires; counting items, persons, and events; and re-

cording information from records. Social measurement tools are usually crude and produce error along with the data.

Measurement is the process of sorting (or mapping) some group of things into the classifications of a variable on the basis of some abstract property. In order to measure you need:

1. Some things to be measured (e.g., responses, people, scores);

2. A variable, with classifications (e.g., "*a*" and "*b*" or "the range from 15 to 50");

3. A definition of an abstract property which some of the things have and others lack, or which they have in varying degree (e.g., persons have lived a number of years; are one sex or another; test scores are high or low);

4. A measurement technique which can determine the extent to which each thing has the property of interest (e.g., you can ask people);

5. A set of guidelines for mapping each thing on the basis of the technique into *one* and *only one* classification of the variable (e.g., if he answers "male," score "1").

For example, if you were examining family incomes, you would have (a) a set of families; (b) a variable: 0–$2,000; $2,001–$5,000; $5,001–$10,000; $10,000 and up; (c) a definition of *family* income which included total cash income earned by all family members; (d) a set of questions you would ask to gain information about family income (e.g., "How much per year do you earn?" and "How much do other members of your family—children, spouse, other family members resident in same household—earn per year?"); (e) the guideline that all reported family income would be summed and the resultant figure place the family in one or another income category. Whatever procedure you use, it must be applied consistently across the total group of things you are measuring even though this group may only be *part* of (or a sample of) a larger group.

Constructing reasonable measures is a very technical and specialized art. Almost anyone can think of questions he would like to ask, but most of these questions would not obtain the desired results. This chapter cannot substitute for experience (in courses or elsewhere) with creating measures; it can only suggest the briefest introduction.

RULE 5.1 As a beginning theorist, use measures that have been used before. If you create or adopt one for use, pretest it thoroughly; consult professional help.

You can assess the reasonableness of any measure you find in the literature by using or thinking about the technique yourself. Can you clearly see the difference between items put into one classification and those put into others? Is the author clear about criteria for these choices? Does the technique map each thing into one and only one classification? For each measure keep track of:

1. The group being measured;
2. The variables created, and the number of classifications of each;
3. The property used by the measurement technique;
4. Details of the technique including (1) guidelines for mapping results into variable classifications, and (2) completeness;
5. Your evaluation of the technique's sensitivity.

You have probably done this sort of evaluation before, and you will improve as you gain experience in handling data. Methods courses and research experience will be invaluable to you.

RULE 5.2 In a dichotomy you need only be able to distinguish "sheep" from "nonsheep"; most measurement techniques are adequate for that task.

EXAMPLE. For the concept "decentralization," we might establish two categories for the associated variable: (1) one decision center, (2) more than one decision center (place a response of "other" in this classification). The measurement derives from answers to questions about who has made an organization's past decisions. If a respondent tells you that one person or one very small cluster of persons (2 to 10) has made all decisions, place your data in class 1; if he indicates more than one, utilize class 2; if the response is ambiguous, place the data in class 2.

MARGINALS

The number of cases in each category of a variable after the measurement of a particular set of cases constitutes the *marginals* for that variable. For example, in a study done just prior to the 1968 election, the interviewer was asked to record the sex of the respondent.[1] There were 1673 respondents in this set of cases. Table 5.1 shows the marginals for categories of the variable 0 and 1, labeled "male" and "female."

Table 5.1 Sex of Respondents

Concept Label	Variable Category	Number	Percentage*
Male	0	726	43.3
Female	1	947	56.6
Total		1673	

* Due to rounding, figures do not add up to 100%.

In the same interview, respondents were asked, "In what social class do you think other people would place you?" Answers of "lower class" or "poor class" were measured as variable category 0; "working," 1; "middle," 2; "upper," 3; and all other responses, 4. Table 5.2 shows the marginals for these categories.

Marginals can help you to make some useful judgments quickly. First, if there are cases in more than one category of the variable, they can demonstrate that your variables do indeed vary; if only males had responded to the study discussed above, the variable would not vary. Second, by demonstrating how the measurement technique works for a particular set of cases, the marginals can give you more insight into broader use of the technique. The sum of the marginals should equal the number of cases; if it does not, the technique is in

[1] Data from the University of Michigan's Survey Research Center, 1968 Presidential Election Survey, on file in Project IMPRESS at Dartmouth College.

Table 5.2 Class of Respondents (Self-report)

Concept Label	Variable Category	Number	Percentage*
Lower	0	19	1.1
Working	1	678	40.5
Middle	2	676	40.4
Upper	3	21	1.2
Other (includes "refused to answer," "don't know," and "no answer")	4	279	16.5
Total		1673	

* Due to rounding, figures do not add up to 100%.

error, either in measurement or reporting. Other uses for marginals will appear in a good methods book such as those listed at the end of this chapter.

FUNCTION

Before you can have a function, you must have two measured variables. A function describes a summary of the particular set of cases measured simultaneously on those two or more variables. A function can be compared with chance or with some other function. For example, the two variables (sex and class) we examined in the preceding section might be described by a frequency table[2] (see Table 5.6) or by one of several other functions (see below).

PROPERTIES AND TYPES OF FUNCTIONS

Any investigator can choose among many possible functions (measures of association) between two variables. Functions vary in form, but

1. They all have a maximum value (usually set to coincide with strong association) and a minimum (usually set to coincide with a finding of random association, i.e., no association, and set at 0).
2. Many functions also have a sign $(+, -)$ attached which indicates whether the values of two associated variables

[2] A frequency table is a necessary precursor to computing any non-scale function. It is the cross-classification of two or more variables.

tend to have the same or a different sign. If the variable values tend to have the same sign, the function is usually positive; if different, negative. For example, if we have set male as $+$ and female, $-$; lower class as $-$, and upper class, $+$; and if males tend to be lower class and females upper class, the sign of the function between sex and class will be $-$.

3. Some functions also have a number which reports strength of association; a high number usually reports strong association, and 0 reports no association (for example, see use of gamma, below, p. 79).

4. Some functions also have an asymmetry associated with them; thus the order in which variables are introduced into the equations which operationalize these functions can affect the outcomes.

5. Another group of functions can be used on three or more variables simultaneously to report the effect of one variable on another, controlling for one or more other variables (control as here used means statistically eliminating the effects of other variables). (For example, see pp. 102–105 in Chapter 6.)

6. Another group of functions can be used only on scale variables while others are specific for nonscale variables (see discussion below of scale variables).

7. A final group specifically reports a total rate of change between two or more variables. If, for example, you had data on age and income for a group of people, you might want to describe how income changed with age.

Table 5.3 summarizes the properties of some types of indices used as functions, and names one example of each type.

You will discover (Chapter 6) that the testing of theories built on causal models such as we are discussing requires that you control for third variables. Thus results from measures of normality, association, or even two-variable correlation are of only small interest. Systematic manipulation of the tables being analyzed produces an approximation to control for third variables using measures of association (Davis, 1971; Goodman and Kruskal, 1954). For the most part, however,

Table 5.3   Properties of Some Types of Indices Used as Functions

Indices of	Sign	Strength	Asymmetry	Control	Scale Variables	Rate of Change
Independence (chi-square)	0*	0	0	0	0	0
Association (gamma)	+	S	0	0	0	0
Partial association (partial correlation, lambda)	+	+	S	+	0	0
Regression (linear regression)	+	+	+	0	+	0
Partial regression (path analysis)	+	+	+	+	+	0
Change (differential equations)	+	+	+	+	+	+

*Key: 0 indicates that the index will *not* show this property.
  + indicates that the index *will* show this property.
  S indicates that the index *may* show this property.

information on functions collected from other peoples' data will only be indicative of the functions that you will need in your own theory.

If you have specific questions about specific functions, or wish to pursue the subject in more detail, many statistics books offer descriptions of assumptions, computing forms, and interpretation of results for many different functions. The Bibliography at the end of this chapter lists some examples.

USE OF NONSCALE FUNCTIONS

For any kind of nonscale function (see Chapter 2, p. 12, for definition), you might translate data from your sources into a frequency table on which you can compute one of the functional indices discussed above. If you have two variables and a set of cases classified on both simultaneously with n categories of variable one and m categories of variable two, you can set up an n by m dummy table in anticipation of your data. Table 5.4 is such a dummy table. Table 5.5 uses the marginals for each of the two variables discussed in the Marginals section to fill in the total marginal frequencies for each category. These indicate the probable size of the frequencies within each cell.

Table 5.4 Dummy Table

	Lower	Working	Middle	Upper	Other	Total
Male						
Female						
Total						

Table 5.5 Dummy Table with Marginals

	Lower	Working	Middle	Upper	Other	Total
Male						726
Female						947
Total	19	678	676	21	279	1673

Table 5.6 is the frequency table with all data entered. Such a table constitutes the basis for computing an index of any nonscale function. The computation of any particular index may require combining categories or manipulating tables, but the frequency table is the basic data source for any computation you might make.

Table 5.6 Frequency Table

	Lower	Working	Middle	Upper	Other	Total
Male	5	310	290	6	115	726
Female	14	368	386	15	164	947
Total	19	678	676	21	279	1673

We now compute two summary statistics of different kinds on this table, chi-square and gamma. Chi-square is 5.578 with 3 degrees of freedom; this figure is small enough to indicate that the two variables are statistically independent. Gamma is 0.05; its small size indicates, as we might expect, that there is little association between sex and perceived class.

RULE 5.3   Collect any frequency tables possible from your sources.

FUNCTIONS BETWEEN SCALE VARIABLES

A scale variable is assumed to be continuous over its range (see Chapter 2, p. 12). Therefore, unless you convert it to a nonscale variable establishing cut points (for example, dividing salary into two categories, "over $10,000" and "$10,000 and under"), you can't use a frequency table to report the data for scale variables. If you want to know whether any pattern of association exists between two scale variables, you must first graph your data. For example, if we graphed age and income data for 100 employed men, we might obtain a scatterplot like Figure 5.1. Either the scatterplot itself, a list

Figure 5.1 Example of a Scatterplot

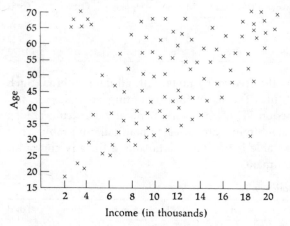

Income (in thousands)

of the data composing it, or a series of descriptive statistics (e.g., the mean, the variance, the standard deviation) would be useful. From the scatterplot you can determine quickly whether any relation exists. If it does, it may be positive (both variables increasing or decreasing simultaneously as in Figure 5.1) or negative (variables moving in opposite directions).

Scales require (or permit) a class of functions different from those suitable for a limited number of classifications. In general, scale functions are more mathematically interesting and tractable. For the level of theory you are constructing with this book, you will not need to use scales and scale functions.

You may, however, find a few in the data of some social scientists, especially demographers and economists.

INDEX VARIABLES

Functions have one further complexity that we should consider. A variable is frequently linked one-to-one with a concept (indeed I have suggested that that is the proper way to link them). But several variables may also be combined in one index variable which has a definitional link to one concept. If you have an index variable, you must also have functions which describe each of the $n \times m$ possible mutual values of the two variables in terms of values of the index variables. You will find such index variables particularly useful when considering key concepts for which it is difficult to find simple variables.

For example, if you were considering the concept "social standing," you might create an index variable running from 0 to 5 to describe the combination of the variables "salary" and "number of club memberships."

Table 5.7 is an example of such an index. To find the information you need, locate the appropriate row and column and then read the index at their point of intersection. For example, you can learn the social standing index (3) of a person belonging to two clubs and earning a salary of $8,000 by locating the intersection of "Two or less" clubs with "$7,000–$9,999" on the table.

Other indices are created by adding the results of the two variables or using some other, more complex, mathematical manipulation of the results of the two (or more) variables. The index will behave in the same way as a regular variable.

Table 5.7 Social Standing Index

Club Membership	Salary			
	$10,000+	$7,000–$9,999	$3,000–$6,999	Under $3,000
Three or more	5	4	3	2
Two or less	4	3	2	1
None	3	2	1	0

STANDARDS

Functions summarize the empirical associations between two variables, sometimes considering and sometimes not considering the effect of other variables. Relations between concepts report the associations expected from a conceptual model, that is, relations are to functions as concepts are to variables. The standard defines how functions and relations fit together.

Let us consider two situations. In the first you have a statistical relation (see Chapter 4) between concepts A and B, and a set of data about variables 1 and 2 which have previously been defined, respectively, with concepts A and B. And you have selected for use a function, Q (one of the various measures of association). As you examine the specifications for Q and the sample sizes for your data you decide that, if for 1 and 2 Q is above .1 or below —.1, the function between those two variables is nonrandom. The standard you state, then, is: "If for 1 and 2 Q_{12} is over ($>$) .1 or less than ($<$) —.1, the data supports my theoretical statement of a relation between concepts A and B."

In the second case, you have data and a proposed function which you want to compute. The function this time is also Q_{12}, and you know that Q carries a sign as well as a statement of nonrandomness. You then state a standard: "If Q is above .1, the evidence suggests an associative, positive relation between A and B; if between .1 and —.1, A and B are not related; and if between —.1 and —1.0, the relation is associative and negatively signed."

Table 5.8 reports the association between properties of functions and relations. You can use it to find an appropriate function for a specific purpose, given that the function must be at least as complex as the relation. For example, if you want a complete test of a signed *relation*, you must choose a function at least as complex as a signed function (e.g., Q); you may use a more complex function (e.g., regression), but to do so will give you more information than you need. If, on the other hand, you started with a regression *function*, you may assert a more detailed (asymmetric, signed) relation between the concepts associated with these variables.

Table 5.8 Relation-Function Properties

Relation Properties	Function Properties
Relation exists	Random-nonrandom (X^2)
Signed	Signed (Q)
Asymetry (causal models)	Controlled (partial regression, partial Q) multiple regression
Strength (path diagrams)	Scale variables (system of equations; regression [partial and multiple])
Time order	Rate of change (differential equation)

You must determine for your theory what function type and strength you will consider sufficient to support any specific assertion of relation. It is necessary to use a consistent standard throughout your theory in order to avoid being charged with making exceptions to include weak, but favorable, associations.

One real difficulty with using standards that occurs when you use other people's results is that, since you are not given a data set but rather a set of calculated results, you cannot do your own data analysis. And these calculations may not control the appropriate variables for your theory. The *pattern* of two-variable associations, however, may help you determine, in a fashion, what *might* be true for a particular association.

If, for example, you have the pattern of two-variable correlations diagrammed in Figure 5.2 and you are interested in the XY association, you can be certain that it cannot be reduced to the point of no significance unless (1) the association is close to begin with, and (2) XZ, ZY are both larger than XY.

Figure 5.2 A Pattern of Correlations

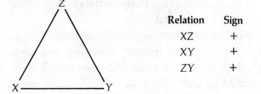

Relation	Sign
XZ	+
XY	+
ZY	+

If, to take another example, two different studies in your collection both contain the same two variables, you might observe whether the signs of the respective functions agree. If they do, the sign of that function in your theory is probably the same as the other two. If they do not, or if the strength of the function is very weak (close to zero), you have no indications at all. In any case, you should collect from your data source, for future analysis by you, any frequency tables that consider two or more variables simultaneously.

Neither of these approaches can substitute for measuring real data, but they do have some indicative value.

RULE 5.4   *a*)   The function and the relation between a concept-variable pair should have similar properties of sign, symmetry, strength, and rate of change.

           b)   If the function and the relation in concept-variable pairs meet your standard with respect to sign, symmetry, strength, and rate, the relation is supported.

Why this elaborate, two-part structure? Why not simply consider the variables and the functions between them? One reason is that the results of two specific studies, even when they replicate exactly the same study design, may show differences in functions between specific variable pairs; the function between two variables might be high in one study and low in another.

The fact of difference itself is not necessarily important. You must determine, however, whether this difference affects your results with respect to the standard you are using. Do the functions from one study support, and those from the other falsify, a relation in your own intellectual structure? If there is a significant difference in the support of your stated relations, that fact is very important; if the difference is small or nonexistent, it can be disregarded.

A second reason for the structure is somewhat more philosophical but perhaps more potent. Strictly speaking, the task of science is to develop an intellectual structure which will order as much of the empirical world as possible. You have now tapped into the body of scientific findings by your selection of sources, and parts of your provisional structure are drawn from others' work. But your provisional structure has an internal logic which will generate new assertions, and some of the old ones are not very well tested. So you must always balance empirical accuracy with theoretical elegance. Only with a two-part structure can we permit free exercise of both accuracy and elegance. The effect of this two-part structure is to reduce the confusion of experience by collapsing those experiences into a smaller number of variables. These variables are then summarized into a smaller number of concepts. And as has been noted before (Chapter 4, pp. 66–67), concepts can be summarized into higher-order concepts.

THE PROTOTHEORY

You began your theory with a pool of quite disconnected, disparate sentences. Some were logical distinctions, others tested propositions, and still others summarized your own observations. The collection of these was not a theory but rather the raw material from which at least one theory could be provisionally constructed. Now you have joined these disparate parts. At several points, lacking means to decide between two alternatives, you have kept both. The whole structure is provisional at this point because it includes many logical holes (a subject to be discussed in Chapter 7) and lacks sufficient empirical testing (Chapter 6) to be called a theory. I call this unit a prototheory to indicate that it is a rough, prior state to a theory.

Only some parts of your prototheory are complete and tested. As you read more social science research literature, you will discover more items needing inclusion in an adequately tested theory. Right now your only certainty is that you have at least one set of possibly consistent, interrelated concepts with a series of alternative formulations for many of the relations. You also have a set of variables which have been linked to these concepts and functions that interrelate these variables at certain points. You also have a standard to determine when function differences indicate differences in relations, and you have developed a specific measurement scheme.

Figure 5.3 is a prototheory model which indicates each part of the prototheory and where discussion of each part occurred in this book. You may find it a quick, handy reference.

Figure 5.3 Complete Skeleton of a Theory

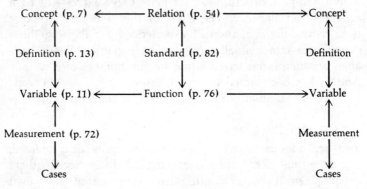

The prototheory itself contains a set of defined concept-variable units which have been linked in at least one simply connected pattern and possibly several alternative patterns. Reducing the number of alternative patterns to one is the primary task of the empirical and logical testing which are your next considerations.

However crude your prototheory is, though, it should be indicative. You should be able to use it in several different ways (to be detailed in the following chapters). And if you work with prototheories for a while, you will get a "feel" for how theories in general work. As problems arise, you will learn how to solve them by elaborating measures, sharpening rules, asserting more complex relations, and so on.

RULES

RULE 5.1 As a beginning theorist, use measures that have been used before. If you create or adopt one for use, pretest it thoroughly; consult professional help.

RULE 5.2   In a dichotomy you need only be able to distinguish "sheep" from "nonsheep"; most measurement techniques are adequate for that task.

RULE 5.3   Collect any frequency tables possible from your sources.

RULE 5.4   *a)* The function and the relation between a concept-variable pair should have similar properties of sign, symmetry, strength, and rate of change.

b) If the function and the relation in concept-variable pairs meet your standard with respect to sign, symmetry, strength, and rate, the relation is supported.

EXERCISES

1. Build from scratch a prototheory about some part of social life that interests you. Begin with concepts and proceed to relations, definitions, variables, proposed functions, measurements, and standards.
2. From a body of data and the variables represented therein, build a prototheory including variables, functions, concepts, definitions, and, using a standard, proposed relations.
3. Using Table 5.7, determine a man's status if he makes $8,310 a year and belongs to three clubs.

BIBLIOGRAPHY

BLALOCK, HUBERT. "The Measurement Problem: A Gap Between the Languages of Theory and Research." In Hubert and Ann Blalock (eds.), *Methodology in Social Research*, pp. 5–27. New York: McGraw-Hill Book Company, 1968.

A more technical but still very readable discussion of problems in putting theory to empirical test.

DAVIS, JAMES A. *Study Design and Data Analysis in Sociology.* Englewood Cliffs, N.J.: Prentice-Hall, Inc., 1971.

An excellent introduction to data analysis. Uses only one,

easy-to-understand function and simplifies measurement and standards for easy understanding.

ELLIS, BRIAN. *Basic Concepts of Measurement.* Cambridge: Cambridge University Press, 1968.

A short, moderately technical and physical science-oriented description of the general properties of measurement.

GOODMAN, LEO A. and WILLIAM H. KRUSKAL. "Measures of Association for Cross Classifications." *Journal of American Statistical Association,* 49 (Dec. 1954), 732–764.

A source and summary of measures of association.

MILLER, DELBERT C. *Handbook of Research Design and Social Measurement.* 2d ed. New York: David McKay Co., Inc., 1970.

A set of more normal measures.

SELLTIZ, CLAIRE, MARIE JAHODA, MORTON DEUTSCH, and STUART W. COOK. *Research Methods in Social Relations.* Rev. 1-vol. ed. New York: Holt, Rinehart and Winston, 1966.

An older book but still very sound, with an emphasis on data collection methods.

SIEGEL, SIDNEY. *Nonparametric Statistics for the Behavioral Sciences.* New York: McGraw-Hill Book Company, 1956.

A statistics cookbook of useful functions for many occasions. Very clearly written and still very good.

WEBB, EUGENE J., DONALD T. CAMPBELL, RICHARD D. SCHWARTZ, and LEE SECHREST. *Unobtrusive Measures: Nonreactive Research in the Social Sciences.* Chicago: Rand McNally and Co., 1966.

A set of measures for unusual situations.

Chapter 6

EMPIRICAL
TESTING

Your prototheory is now as complete a piece of conceptual machinery as you can make it simply by searching sources and adding new concepts (Chapter 2, pp. 7–9) and variables (Chapter 2, pp. 11–13). Your pattern of concepts and relations probably resembles Figure 6.1 (a repeat from Chapter 4). You

Figure 6.1 Complete Berelson and Steiner Theory of Organization: Alternative 1

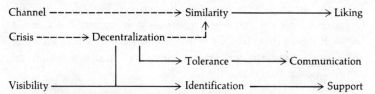

should have proposed more than one alternative approach to ordering the concepts in your prototheory. Figure 6.2 suggests an alternative formulation to 6.1. You might have developed an alternative formulation by:

1. Reading another source with a different theory;
2. Finding a logical inconsistency and developing alternative prototheories around logically consistent alternatives;
3. Thinking about the prototherapy and perceiving new possibilities.

Figure 6.2 Complete Berelson and Steiner Theory of Organization: Alternative 2

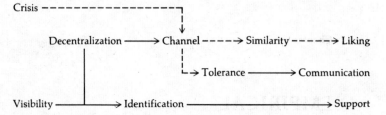

Obviously, if you used many sources and a large set of concepts, you could have many alternative formulations. The concepts in these alternative formulations are associated with each other by relations (Chapter 2, pp. 23–25) and with specific variables by definitions (Chapter 2, pp. 13–18). In your prototheory this set of concept-variable units remains *constant* across all alternative formulations.

This chapter and Chapter 7 will suggest ways to eliminate some of these alternative formulations through empirical and structural testing whose goal is to designate the one best alternative as a provisional theory. Structural testing (to be considered in Chapter 7) evaluates each alternative formulation against minimal and maximal criteria, eliminating or revising those which are unsatisfactory. Empirical testing (considered in this chapter) compares the predictions made by each alternative for the values of functions between variables and eliminates or revises those alternatives which do not fit known functions.

THE TESTING
CYCLE

PRETESTING

Pretesting begins with deducing from the pattern of concepts and relations among them the pattern of functions expected among associated variables. If you have two alternatives (e.g., Figures 6.1 and 6.2), you should watch for aspects of the alternatives which show different concept patterns (e.g., Figure 6.3). Alternative 1 predicts a positive function between

Figure 6.3 Differences in Empirical Prediction Between Alternatives 1 and 2

Alternative 1

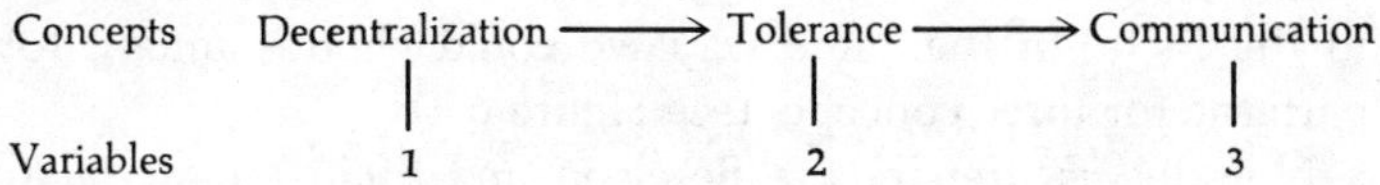

Concepts	Decentralization ——→ Tolerance ——→ Communication
Variables	1 2 3

Alternative 2

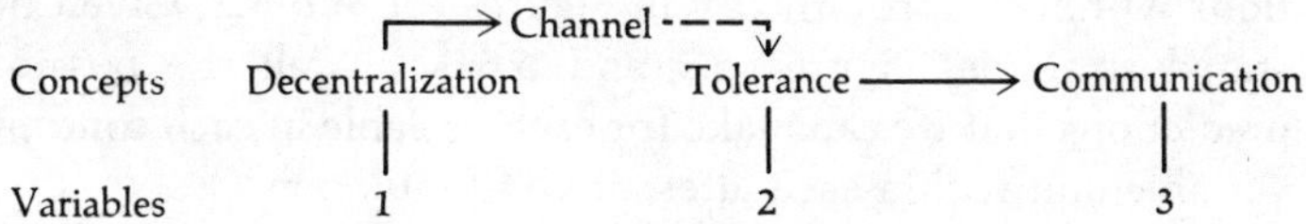

```
               ┌——→ Channel ----┐
                                 v
Concepts   Decentralization      Tolerance ——→ Communication
Variables        1                  2              3
```

Prediction for Function Between Variables

Alternative	1-2	2-3	1-3
1	+	+	+
2	−	+	−

Figure 6.4 Prediction of Function Signs from Prototheory Alternatives

Alternatives*

(1) A ————→ B ————→ C

(2) A ————→ B - - - - - → C

(3) A - - - - - → B ————→ C

(4) A - - - - - → B - - - - - → C

Prediction of Function Between Variables

Alternative	1–2	1–3	2–3
1	+	+	+
2	+	−	−
3	−	+	−
4	−	−	+

*Variable 1 is associated with concept A; 2 with B; and 3 with C.

variables 1 and 2; alternative 2 predicts a negative function. If we measure variables 1 and 2, we can learn what function actually holds and thus discover which alternative is closer to the facts. In the same way we could choose among four patterns for three concepts (see Figure 6.4).

Now let us prepare the Berelson and Steiner material for empirical testing. We already have two alternative formulations within the prototheory in Figures 6.1 and 6.2. Given the stated relations, Figures 6.5 and 6.6 show all the possible predictions that we can make for each variable in each concept-variable unit within each alternative formulation.

If we consider Figure 6.5, case 1, for example, we find that all variables in beginning concept-variable units have "+" values. If we follow out the established definitions and relations we find that the variables defined with "tolerance," "decentralization," and "communication" should have "—"

Figure 6.5 Prediction of Variable Signs for Berelson and Steiner Theory of Organization: Alternative 1

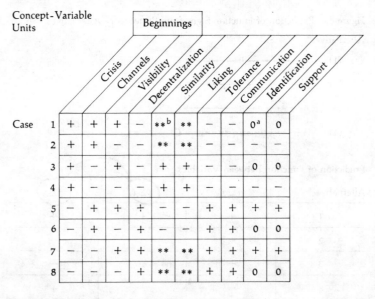

| Concept-Variable Units | | Beginnings | | | | | | | | |
Case	Crisis	Channels	Visibility	Decentralization	Similarity	Liking	Tolerance	Communication	Identification	Support
1	+	+	+	−	**b	**	−	−	0a	0
2	+	+	−	−	**	**	−	−	−	−
3	+	−	+	−	+	+	−	−	0	0
4	+	−	−	−	+	+	−	−	−	−
5	−	+	+	+	−	−	+	+	+	+
6	−	+	−	+	−	−	+	+	0	0
7	−	−	+	+	**	**	+	+	+	+
8	−	−	−	+	**	**	+	+	0	0

a *And* situations; the prediction is zero (see Chapter 4).
b *Or* situations; the theory will not predict (see Chapter 4).

Figure 6.6 Prediction of Variable Signs for Berelson and Steiner Theory of Organization: Alternative 2

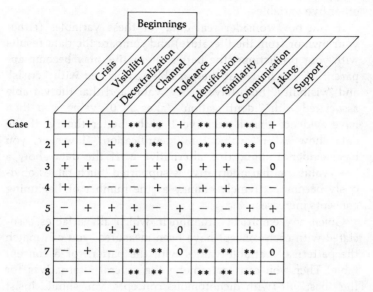

Case	Crisis	Visibility	Decentralization	Channel	Tolerance	Identification	Similarity	Communication	Liking	Support
1	+	+	+	**	**	+	**	**	**	+
2	+	−	+	**	**	0	**	**	**	0
3	+	+	−	−	+	0	+	+	−	0
4	+	−	−	−	+	−	+	+	−	−
5	−	+	+	+	−	+	−	−	+	+
6	−	−	+	+	−	0	−	−	+	0
7	−	+	−	**	**	0	**	**	**	0
8	−	−	−	**	**	−	**	**	**	−

values, while those defined with "identification" and "support" show "0" values. These variables *must* be zero because the relation between "decentralization," "visibility," and "identification" is an *and* relation (symbolized by the joined arrow in 6.1 and discussed in Chapter 4, p. 60). This relation tells us that both "decentralization" and "visibility" are necessary to "identification"; when two necessary prior concepts differ as they do in case 1, we can only assume that the variable will show a "0" value.

Continuing the same case, "similarity" and "liking" are connected by *or* with "crisis" and "channel" (*or* symbolized by two separate arrows to the concept; see Chapter 4, pp. 58–59). When two concepts precede and are joined by *or* to a later concept, we can predict the value of the variable in the later concept-variable unit only when the preceding concepts would independently predict the same value. Otherwise we can make no predictions. Figure 6.6 considers alternative 2. If (case 1) the data show that variables associated with the beginning concept are "+," the predictions for "identification" and "support" will be "+." No predictions are made about the other five variables.

If you now consider real data for these variables (either your own or from the literature) and compare the data results with your predictions, the better alternative may become apparent. If you find that the variables associated with "crisis" and "visibility" both have a "+" value and that the variable associated with "identification" takes a "0" value, you then have evidence that alternative 1 is the better theory. If the data show a "+" value for "identification," however, you have evidence supporting alternative 2. If the data show a "−" value, neither alternative is supported. Such tables obviously become extremely clumsy as the number of beginning concepts increases.

Given any empirical situation in which all variables associated with each concept have been measured, you can match the pattern of variable values with the pattern of a concept table. Then you can sort among the several alternatives for the "best" fit (with dichotomous concepts, you should insist on perfect fit). If the patterns fit perfectly, you have evidence that your alternative is not wrong for this data. It is not necessarily true, either, but it *has* passed one test.

A second test may be possible if you do not know all the values for variables in your concept-variable units. You can trim your prototheory down to include only those concepts for whose variables you have some data. You may then use the sign rule within alternatives to predict values for some of the nonbeginning concept-variable units. If the resultant predictions do not differ from alternative to alternative, however, you obviously cannot test one against the other.

RULE 6.1   Using the sign rule, predict the values of subsequent variables from beginning variable values.

RULE 6.2   A test should distinguish among alternatives.

Here as in Chapter 5, it should be noted that methods and statistics courses or research experience will help you immensely in putting your alternatives to empirical test. This chapter will introduce you to the process, but actual practice is the best teacher.

TESTING

The testing process includes study design, execution, and data analysis. These parts are usually considered in a methods course, and I will therefore limit my discussion to concerns particularly relevant to theory building.

From the viewpoint of theory, testing should avoid creating theoretical errors and be as broad as possible. Error can occur through (1) misclassification of cases into variable categories, (2) miscalculations, (3) wrong analysis (e.g., the use of inappropriate tests), or (4) failure to control other relevant variables.

The first three types of errors are subject to control through methodological rules; methods books suggested in this chapter's Bibliography will indicate how. The last type of error may indicate that your theory is too small or that it lacks adequate concepts. In the prototheory you are testing, the failure of several tests to give similar results is the best indication of uncontrolled variables.

It is generally best to test any theory in an experimental situation. Occasionally in social science (particularly if you are testing the relations among individuals within small groups of persons), experimental situations are possible. Usually, however, we must take data from uncontrolled, nonexperimental situations; difficulties in most social science methods can be traced to this fact. We must, therefore, design our analyses to achieve the best control possible under such circumstances, realizing that we can never achieve the degree of precise control that is so relatively easy for the physical scientist.

You should note that measurements may be made across time (e.g., 10 years ago, 5 years ago, now) in panel or time-series studies; these studies are particularly valuable in testing the assertion of causal order in a theory. You can also measure the differences between social units in comparative studies (e.g., hospitals in Japan and the United States); such studies may indicate new concepts and variables that studies based on one culture would not reveal. The testing of a theory's sensitivity to different factors in new settings is a very important task. Contextual studies (e.g., the effect of a school on its students) offer an excellent way to test for both sensitivity and the psychological effects of a social context. The majority of studies done in the United States are case classificatory (e.g., public opinion survey). These data can measure the function between variables at a single point in time. This variety of techniques, while not compensating totally for the lack of experimentation, does make the testing of prototheories possible.

RULE 6.3   Obtain data from several types of studies.

All aspects of theory and prototheory testing should be open public information. Any time you publish the results of an investigation, refer to your complete report and make it available. Such openness invites critique and allows for use of the theory in ways the theorist might not have foreseen. Particular attention should be paid to the rationale for measurement techniques chosen and to any data not used in analysis.

RULE 6.4   Publicize all measurement and testing techniques, including sources of possible error.

From the theoretical viewpoint, you are not particularly interested in sampling procedures. You should, however, state your theory as generally as possible; for example, you could state it as true for the whole human race. It is unlikely that you could actually study the *whole* human race, but you *can* demonstrate its untruth for the whole human race *if* you have a reasonable sample of some part of it. For example, it is not impossible to have a reasonable sample of American college students. If the relation does not hold for that sample, then the general proposition is in trouble. You could save the proposition by stating it as true for the whole human race, except American college students. Most people, however, would give little weight to any theory stated as universally true—except where it had been tested.

The preceding discussion aside, however, there is little penalty for setting very wide limits and some benefit in that you open wider situations in which to test a proposition. You may even find that some testing has been done. Reasonable units are: a social group (e.g., Catholics), an organization (e.g., Knights of Columbus), a geographical area (e.g., Great Plains), a political entity (e.g., the state of Illinois), or some combination of these (e.g., all Illinois Catholics who belong to the Knights of Columbus). If you find different samples producing different test results, then you should try to isolate the specific factors within sampling groups that are affecting the variables under scrutiny.

RULE 6.5 Obtain your sample cases from as comprehensive a unit as possible.

INDETERMINANCY

If a test of your alternatives clearly shows either that the associations are *not* as you had hypothesized or that one is clearly accurate, you can proceed with little difficulty. The usual (and exasperating) case in research, however, is that you are never sure because the data neither quite prove nor disconfirm any single alternative within your prototheory. Such indeterminancy can happen for a number of reasons. Among them:

1. The only available data does not distinguish between (among) your alternatives. For example, if you had data only on "crisis," "identification," and "decentralization" for a series of organizations, you would be unable to decide whether alternative 1 or alternative 2 was closer to the facts.

2. The functions, although correctly signed, are very close to your standard (e.g., 1.2 when your standard is 1.1). A series of function confirmations very close to your standard does not strongly support your theory.

Under these circumstances you should:

1. Report the situation fully. Include a summary of alternatives, data source searched, and tests carried out.

2. Suggest what someone else might do to make the situa-

tion more determinant (e.g., specific research may be required).

3. Proceed either to follow your own suggestions or to work on some other theory.

The social nature of science is clearest when you realize that you need not finish a particular project although you might wish to do so. That piece of research might better be left for someone else who is better equipped to complete it.

EVALUATION

As a beginning theorist you will be able to evaluate your test procedures only insofar as they grossly conform to the measurement specifications you set. And you should remember that, while a test may prove the inadequacy of a particular part of your prototheory, it may also simply reflect an inadequacy in your testing procedure. Alternatives within a prototheory are provisional; any that you or I or any other social analyst generates will likely contain some error. A perfect fit, for other than a theory composed of dichotomous concept-variable units, is unlikely and any such fit should be distrusted.

Two imperfections are common: (1) measurement errors and (2) incompleteness. In advanced theories each variable is accompanied by an error term which indicates how much of a variable's variance can be attributed to the explicit previous variables, how much to measurement error, and how much to uncontrolled variation.[1]

COSTS

Testing takes time and costs money; both factors limit the kinds of testing you can do. As you experiment with different tests, you will learn to judge the amounts of time and money needed to do them (and by the way, the time and money need not necessarily be yours). Testing can be the most stimulating part of the whole sociological enterprise because, if your ideas are interesting, others will join you in research and testing.

When you test a prototheory, you will often find that

[1] For readers familiar with statistical regression technique, H. Blalock's *Theory Construction* deals very fully with error terms and error estimation.

the dollar costs of research permit only a small study. One nondollar cost of doing a small study, however, is that you thereby limit the number of concept-variable units you can test. The number of cases you consider (N) ought (minimally) to be roughly five times the product of all categories $[5(c_1)(c_2) \ldots (c_n)]$. For example, the N for a five-variable block where all variables are dichotomous ought to be $[5(2)(2)(2)(2)(2)] = 160$. If you include this many cases and set reasonable cutting points for your variables,[2] your sample will be adequate.

RULE 6.6   *a*) Consider cost factors when testing. Use others' data analysis and aid where you can.

          b) Choose enough cases to test your theory but not so many as to be wasteful.

If your prototheory fails, you need to know what failed and why. Failure suggests possible activities: reformulation, dropping the whole enterprise, major revision. How do you decide which? Check your theory. Are the errors concentrated in one branch or part of it? Are they the result of one premise that might be modified? If your failure has resulted from the misprediction of one or two relations, you may be able to save the theory. If errors exist in several parts of the theory with no obvious connection among them, either make major changes or scrap the theory and quit. Only with experience will you be able to judge whether a flaw is fatal. You should report fully your failures as well as successes. Indeed, failures may constitute the most important part of your report.

REVISING A PROTOTHEORY

FUNCTIONS

Statistical testing is a variety of analysis known to most advanced students. If a function exists between two variables,

---

[2] If the marginals for your variables are close to equal size, you have set reasonable cutting points. If they are not and some of them are very small, you will have to reset cutting points to increase the number of cases in the smaller categories.

then variation in one is likely to produce a predictable variation in the second. All of the more complicated statements in science are based on this fact of association.

If you are questioning a function and your research is experimental, you should repeat the experiment on more subjects. If the same results reappear, your belief in the relationship's existence will be strengthened. If your study is a survey, you can frequently obtain more data either with more cases or with another survey. If you doubt your results and cannot increase the size of your sample, however, then you must turn to statistical testing for help.

The difficulty with statistical testing has been that the emphasis on testing for the existence of association or differences per se has drawn attention away from the *strength* or *size* of these associations. Yet it is true that weak associations or small differences may simply not be very important. Too often research literature will assure you that a function exists between two variables but give you no estimates of its strength.

To evaluate the strength of a function, examine the accuracy of prediction yielded. There are many tests for accuracy of prediction (e.g., variance explained). If, for example, a particular examination gives 80 percent predictive accuracy and if without the exam you predict with 60 percent accuracy, you can conclude that the examination helps and that the association between test score and success is quite strong. Statistical testing is a pretty inelegant business, though, and conclusions are not handed to you by statistical procedures.

A series of sociological evaluation procedures have developed over the last several years. Figure 6.7 summarizes some of these, indicating their sources, distinguishing characteristics, and the person most identified with their development in sociology. The function type that you choose to test data against an alternative in your prototheory will be determined by your relation type (see Chapter 5, pp. 76–81).

An analyst's job is not finished when he has tested his prototheory. He must also search for other truths in the data. What assertions and implications can be drawn that were previously unseen? In the final analysis, you have only your judgment to rely on when you generalize. When you move beyond the confines of your central model, you should restate the conditions under which a stated relation should be expected to recur.

Figure 6.7 Styles of Search in Theory*

	Characteristic	Person**	System Type	Sources
Sophistication	Propositions	Homans (1950) Zetterberg (1962)	Two-variable propositions Logical deduction	Philosophy
	Partialing	Lazarsfeld (1954)	Survey control of test variables	
	System of variables	Davis (1971)	Simple causal models	
	Graphs + linear equation translations	Stinchcombe (1968)	Signal graphs	Huggins and Entwistle (1968) Electrical engineering
	Error terms Identification problems	Blalock (1964)	Linear systems Spurious correlation	Simon (1957) Economic models
	Measurement of relationships	Duncan (1966)	Path analysis	Wright (1934) Genetics
	Nonrecursive models	Blalock (1969)	Differential equations	Wold (1953) Econometrics
	Nonlinear models		Differential equations	

*This is not intended to be complete, only suggestive.

**See Bibliography for complete references.

Remember that all testing procedures are based on the fact that we can find associations between (among) variables. There are always other variables that have associations and that could have effects were they to change. In no sense can you ever "close off" a situation and guarantee that your test results will always hold. Even physical science experimentation assumes variables (e.g., the force of gravity, air pressure) that are controlled or can be assumed not to change from one time to the next.

Ceteris paribus really means that if certain variables not included in a system are proven to have a major effect on the theory's central variables, the theorist cannot be blamed. One major object of science is to "capture" as many as possible of these variables in a theory.

STANDARDS

The standard we discussed in Chapter 5 was a simple one. Identical signs on the function and the relation between two concept-variable pairs indicated that the relation was not disconfirmed. We were limited to those cases in which both the function and the relation were signed, whether or not the function was asymmetric. We could test the sign, but not the direction, of a causal relation with a correlation coefficient or some other function. If the sign of the function and the relation were different, that fact *disconfirmed* the stated relation.

This standard presents two difficulties. First, how do you test asymmetric relations for a fit with functions? Second, how do you avoid obtaining incorrect readings from your standard when your set of variables is incomplete? You can test most efficiently by testing a whole system of variables for their fit to a whole alternative in your prototheory. To do this testing properly, you need more statistical sophistication than can be provided here. I refer you to Davis (1971) and Blalock (1969) for further information.

Even when a relation is confirmed, you should be alert to the possibility of hidden factors working within a particular situation. Sometimes you will find strong, two-variable functions to which you can assign no meaning, for example, "Single people eat more candy than married people." What does this function mean? Candy eating certainly does not cause people to be single. Does being single cause people to eat candy? This mystery disappears when we control for age (a previously "hidden factor"); we then find that the function between marriage and candy is zero (see Zeisel, 1957, p. 198). In experimentation one tries to remove the possibility of hidden factors by controlling and randomizing. In nonexperimental research, however, the researcher cannot alter the conditions under which data are collected; at best he can try to hold conditions statistically constant.

The theoretical questions raised by hidden factors are: (1) What variables should an investigator try to control? (2) How many variables should he study? An investigator normally begins with those variables that the concepts of his theory indicate as holding *intervening positions* (i.e., between beginning and ending variables); he then checks alternatives that his good sense and imagination suggest might be useful. Finally he considers those variables indicated as relevant by some data. The actual number of variables considered is limited only by cost. A theorist should check those variables that occur in his theory, but he can never try all the possible variables, and he can never be certain that he has included in his theory all the relevant ones. The more variables he tries, however (assuming they are carefully chosen), the more certain he can be that any specific function in his prototheory is indeed a significant one.

An example of a hidden third factor can be found in the relation between economists' education and salary. Common sense suggests that more education should result in a higher salary:

$$\text{education} \rightarrow \text{salary}$$

Table 6.1 shows median salaries paid to economists who have completed different levels of education. With the exception of the Ph.D degree, it appears that an economist's salary will

Table 6.1 Salaries of Economists at Different Education Levels, 1966*

Degree	Median Reported Salary
Ph.D.	$13,500
Master's	12,000
Bachelor's	14,700
Less than bachelor's	16,500

* Source: National Science Foundation, *American Science Manpower 1966*, p. 92.

vary inversely with the amount of education he has, yet common sense judges this situation quite improbable. A theorist would guess that education would still have some causal effect on salary if another variable (i.e., employment) were considered simultaneously. And this proves to be the case (see Table 6.2).

Table 6.2 Salaries of Economists,
By Degree and Type of Employer, 1966*

Degree and Type of Employer	Median Annual Salary
Educational institutions	
Ph.D. degree	$14,000
Master's degree	10,500
Bachelor's degree	11,900
Federal government	
Ph.D. degree	16,200
Master's degree	13,800
Bachelor's degree	13,400
Other governments	
Ph.D. degree	16,600
Master's degree	11,500
Bachelor's degree	12,000
Nonprofit organizations	
Ph.D. degree	18,500
Master's degree	14,000
Bachelor's degree	14,000
Industry-business	
Ph.D. degree	20,000
Master's degree	14,000
Bachelor's degree	15,000
Less than Bachelor's degree	18,000
Self-employed	
Master's degree	18,000
Bachelor's degree	18,000

* Source: National Science Foundation, *American Science Manpower 1966*, p. 92.

Table 6.2 cross-classifies by type of employer. Within each type of employment, amount of education and salary are positively associated. Taken together, then, amount of education and type of employment yield a better and more sensible cause-and-effect relationship than either variable does alone. (One indicator that the explanation is better is that the range of salaries among amounts of education within each type of employment is greater than the range when amounts of education alone are considered.)

This example is interesting because the original function is reversed; the simple association shows an inverse relationship between education and salary, whereas the refined association is positive. This example shows the wisdom of further exploration into some negative or "zero" relationships, especially when the observed association does not make very good common sense or fit well with your prototheory.[3]

The direction of a relation can be checked by complementary methods: (1) reasoning and general knowledge (including knowledge of time order), and (2) pattern of implications that the theory produces. For example, a concept-variable unit is unlikely to be placed at the beginning of a theory if the variable has 0 functions with every other variable.

After analyzing sign and direction, you can investigate the strength of an association. Crude levels were set when you stated what actual correlation figures you would set as your standard for positive, negative, and zero correlations. We often set purely arbitrary standards (e.g., .1 or above) for confirmation (in the sense that this is a size to be concerned about) and disconfirmation (e.g., below .1 is effectively zero).

As you increase the number of relation levels and measure functions more and more precisely, you will need a more complex, complete, and precise standard to specify exactly what state of which function is confirming what state of which relation. The standard then becomes a statement (probably mathematical) of the association between function solutions for particular data and relation assertions for the applicable alternative in your prototheory.

RULES

RULE 6.1 Using the sign rule, predict the values of subsequent variables from beginning variable values.

[3] This example adapted from J. Simon (1969), p. 355.

RULE 6.2   A test should distinguish among alternatives.

RULE 6.3   Obtain data from several types of studies.

RULE 6.4   Publicize all measurement and testing techniques, including sources of possible error.

RULE 6.5   Obtain your sample cases from as comprehensive a unit as possible.

RULE 6.6   *a*) Consider cost factors when testing. Use others' data analysis and aid where you can.

   b) Choose enough cases to test your theory but not so many as to be wasteful.

EXERCISES

1. *a*) Pick a proposition you do not believe. Propose a test for it.
     (1) Give operations so that the meanest intelligence could discern the state of your variables.
     (2) State what you expect to find.
     (3) Pick an outcome that would cause you to rewrite your proposition. Show what you would do with it.
   b) Pick a proposition that is quite believable and repeat the above.
   c) Give three alternatives for the phenomena you are trying to explain. Call them A, B, C. List the tests which would permit you to tell A from B, B from C, and A from C.
   d) On what unit would you test these alternatives?
2. Choose any relation between two or more variables of some social interest and in which you are personally interested; invent at least three prototheories of at least five variables not now known to be false which might explain these relations. Choosing appropriate indicators, derive at least three different empirical consequences from each prototheory such that the factual consequences distinguish among the theories.

BIBLIOGRAPHY

BLALOCK, HUBERT. *Theory Construction: From Verbal to Mathematical Formulations.* Englewood Cliffs, N.J.: Prentice-Hall, Inc., 1969.

   Testing for the advanced student; Blalock assumes familiarity with multiple regression techniques.

BLALOCK, HUBERT. *An Introduction to Social Research.* Englewood Cliffs, N.J.: Prentice-Hall, Inc., 1970.

   An elementary discussion of testing, written in Blalock's usual clear style.

DAVIS, JAMES A. *Study Design and Data Analysis in Sociology.* Englewood Cliffs, N.J.: Prentice-Hall, Inc., 1971.

   Testing for the novice.

PHILLIPS, BERNARD S. *Social Research: Strategy and Tactics.* New York: The Macmillan Company, 1966.

   An easy introduction to general problems of social research.

SIMON, JULIAN L. *Basic Research Methods in Social Science: The Art of Empirical Investigation.* New York: Random House, 1969.

   A very good discussion of social science techniques at a more advanced level than Phillips.

Chapter 7

STRUCTURAL
TESTING

Theories should pass both empirical and structural tests and should be retested both ways until one clear, satisfactory alternative exists which can be termed a provisional theory. Your prototheory may or may not have passed some empirical tests before you begin structural testing. Structural testing compares alternatives within a prototheory for their approximation first to minimal and then to maximal criteria for theory. In addition to structural testing, this chapter also considers ways to revise the parts of your prototheory by eliminating difficulties you have discovered in testing.

MINIMAL CRITERIA:
   VAGUENESS AND
      CONTRADICTION

Your prototheory probably contains vagueness and internal contradiction. You must correct these inadequacies if any alternatives are to meet the minimal criteria for good theory.

Vagueness and sometimes contradiction may occur because concepts derive from specific symbol systems which are not necessarily consistent with each other. With variables the difficulty is precision with respect to measurement (see later discussion in this chapter). But variables are only categories named for convenience; they are not part of a language or pattern of understanding. With concepts, definitions must be part of and consistent with a symbol system. Many symbol systems may be involved, each the property of a community that supports it through conceptual machinery and cognitive and normative grammars. Figure 7.1 diagrams some of the

Figure 7.1 The Communities of a Theorist

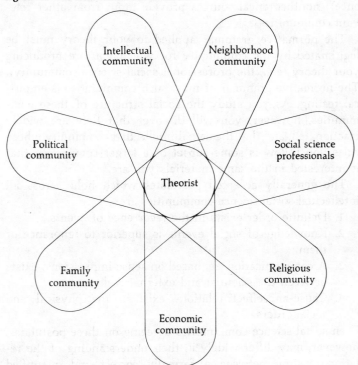

communities in which a theorist as human being may live. Each community, including the intellectual ones shown, may overlap in (a) personnel (other than the focal person); (b) symbol content (of which structural testing is a part); (c) style of normative grammar; and/or (d) style of cognitive grammar (of which logical testing is a part). The latter three are discussed in Berger and Luckmann, 1966. When you use various materials as the sources of your theory, you are really searching the various communities to which you and the authors belong for the content of their symbolic universes. You subsequently use this content to operate concepts in another universe, that of systematic social analysis. Thus a source in already existing theory provides input from one relevant intellectual community (e.g., social theorists' experience); nontheoretical sources provide input from other relevant communities.

The normative grammar applied to your theory must be legitimated by the community for which you are producing your theory (e.g., the professional social science community). The normative grammar of most such communities is empirical testing. As you study the social structure of these communities, however, you will discover that they are widely fractionated, and that the actual intellectual community whose rules you follow is some subset of a larger community that is interested in the same materials you are.

The generally accepted postulates which hold across all intellectual social science communities are:

1. Definite order exists in the recurrence of events.
2. Knowledge of social events is superior to ignorance of them.
3. A communication tie, based on sense impressions, exists between the scientist and external reality.
4. Cause-and-effect relations exist in the physical and social orders.

Even social science communities agreeing on these postulates, however, may differ widely in their understanding of the relation existing between a formally correct and quantified variable and the much less precise, often wordy, concept.

Indeed, vagueness frequently occurs not just in the concept but in the concept-variable unit, and this lack of clarity may exist because your material came from several different sources. The connection between one author's concept and the variables measured by a second may not have been clear, and your definition may not have clarified the connection between them. In particular, your definitions must be consistent. Definitions with dichotomous variables are consistent if a "+" on variable 1 is defined onto its associated concepts so that a positive relation between concept 1 and concept 2 implies a "+" on variable 2. For variables with more classifications whose associated concepts relate positively, a "high" on variable 1 should imply a "high" on variable 2. If your definitions and measurement procedures are completely clear (i.e., your concepts and variables are composed of complete and exclusive classifications and categories), then your concept-variable units are not vague. If vagueness seems to persist (for example, a variable's categories seem to overlap), you might consider making two or more concepts or two or more variables out of the original, each containing one of the possible meanings.

Internal contradictions exist if the implications from two different premises within an alternative disagree, or if the implications from one premise disagree directly with another premise. The simplest case is a triad of concepts, *A,B,C*, represented in Figure 7.2.

Figure 7.2 Inconsistent Relations

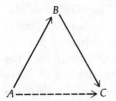

The path *ABC* implies that *AC* is positive, yet the direct relation is negative. These paths contradict each other; in these models the same relation *cannot* take both signs. Given this situation, you have two choices. You can build two consonant models (see Figure 7.3) and test these as alternatives. Or you can build a more complex model, in which the effects of the implied and direct (or of several direct) relations may be taken into account separately (see below).

If the alternative you finally select from your prototheory is neither vague nor internally contradictory, you then have

Figure 7.3 Resolution of Inconsistent Relations

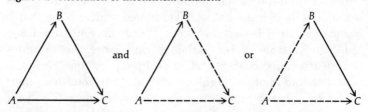

a minimal theory (i.e., an acceptable effort, but not the best you can do).

RULE 7.1 Remove vagueness from your prototheory by producing two or more clear, alternative statements from that vagueness.

RULE 7.2 Resolve internal contradiction by:
  a) developing alternatives, each of which is internally consistent; *or*
  b) building a more complex model.

MINIMAL CRITERIA:
CONTRADICTION
RESOLUTION

You have been using asymmetric, signed, associational, deterministic, transitive relations without an indicator of relational strength. A relation without strength indicated permits only a statement of association (or nonassociation) and the sign of that association. For example, if concepts *A* and *B* are both related to concept *C* (as in Figures 7.2 or 7.3), then (1) the direct effects of all relations coming to each concept must agree on sign if you are to avoid indeterminancy or a zero sign (Chapter 4, pp. 58–60), and (2) the direct and implied relations must show the same sign if you are to avoid internal contradiction (as in Figure 7.2 discussed above).

You may eliminate some internal contradiction rather easily by changing from deterministic to statistical theory (see Chapter 4, pp. 55–56). The effect of this change is to give all implications a different status from assertions (or direct relations). The change in status makes implications tentative and their disagreement with assertions quite acceptable. There are costs to such a change; statistical theory does not resolve contradictory direct effects any better than the deterministic theory we have been using. More important, statistical theory lacks the chains of implication that make deterministic theory exciting. The implications of statistical theory are few; and those implications make no further implications (Chapter 4, pp. 56–57).

STRENGTH IN RELATIONS

A more useful procedure is to retain the deterministic character of your theory and to add a statement of relative strength to each relation. You can make this addition by stating what percentage (e.g., 30 percent), usually expressed as a decimal (.30), of the total concept under consideration is attributable to each of the "causing" concepts. In Figure 7.4, for example,

Figure 7.4 Strength Graph of Five Concepts

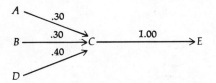

we state that A causes .30 of C; B, .30; and D, .40. Now consider E. C is related 1.0 with E, and the theory implies that A, B, and D all relate to E by implication. The relation of A to E must be connected with the direct relations of A to C and C to E. I am proposing that the connection is the *product* of those two direct relations; thus $AE = AC \times CE$ (Huggins and Entwisle, 1968).

In general you can use the process described with the following example to find the strength of the implication between any two concepts. To determine total relation (direct and indirect) between y and t of the theory shown in Figure 7.5a where $A_1 A_2 \ldots A_6$ are the relations and w, x, y, z and t are concepts, you need only "absorb" the appropriate concepts between them. To absorb concepts, add the effects of two arrows entering a concept and multiply sequential arrows. If we begin by absorbing "w," we obtain Figure 7.5b. In removing "z" we must multiply the arrow from "x" times the arrow to "t" and then add the direct "xt" arrow. The result is in Figure 7.5c. We can finish by noting that "y" has two channels to "t," one direct, and one through "x." The result is Figure 7.5d. The final effect of "y" on "t" is shown in Figure 7.5e.

Figure 7.5 Summarizing the Relations Between y and t

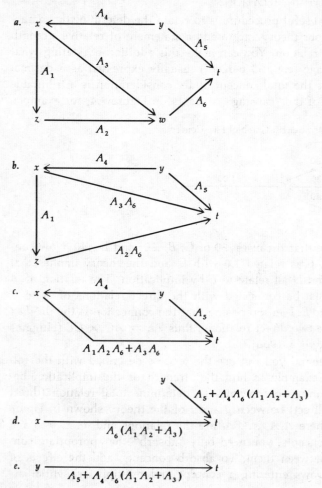

To determine the numerical size of each A, we must find the size of some A's since we have fewer equations than unknowns. To find the numerical size of y's effect on t, we need to know the sizes of A_2 and A_3 as well as A_5 and A_6. We know that A_2 and A_3 add up to 1.0, as do A_5 and A_6. We also know that A_4 and A_1 are 1.0 because no other relations come to x and z respectively.

Let us arbitrarily state that $A_2 = .4$ and $A_5 = .5$; these statements will determine $A_3 = .6$ and $A_6 = .5$. Figure 7.6

Figure 7.6 Numerical Example of a Strength Graph

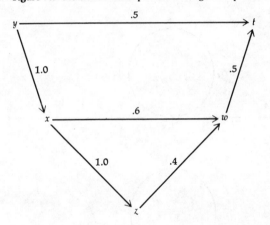

describes the situation. The indirect effect of z on t, given these statements, is .2 (i.e., .4 times .5); of x on t is .3 (i.e., .6 times .5). This technique permits you to resolve both direct and indirect inconsistency.

LOOPS

This technique also provides a way for you to assess transmission in graphs including a loop, often the case with time-bound theories (see Chapter 4, p. 68). Figure 7.7*a* shows the simplest case, a graph from u to v with a loop at "t." In 7.7*b* we eliminate the point "w," leaving a graph with a loop going from and returning to the same point. The effect of a loop with a strength indicator can be shown to be 1/(1-indicator) (see Huggins and Entwisle). For clarity we can separate "t" into "input to t" (called here t') and "output from t" and designate the loop at "t" the direct connecting relation. This operation gives us graph 7.7c, a linear graph in the normal form which we can now easily reduce to Figure 7.7d.

Stinchcombe's discussion of linear graphs (1968, pp. 39–148) points out that, although graphs with loops are intuitively appealing because they facilitate the graphing of functional and homeostatic theories, the testing of such theories

Figure 7.7 Summarizing the Relations Between u and v with an Intervening Loop

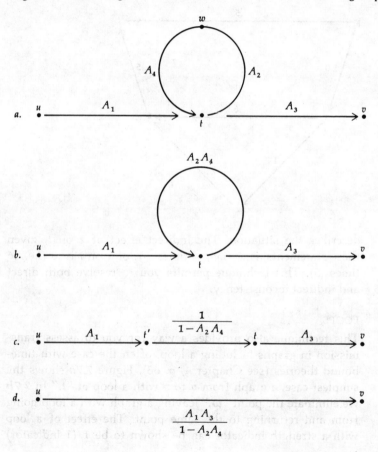

is nevertheless very difficult. Blalock's *Theory Construction* indicates that calculus offers a way to develop functions which test theories with loops in them. A theory including a loop with concept relations and functions actually discovered has not, to my knowledge, been developed for a nonhypothetical example.

RULE 7.3 Resolve contradictory direct and indirect relations by assigning relative strength indicators to relations.

RULE 7.4 *a*) The indirect effect of any concept on any other can be computed by multiplying the indicators along any path and adding separate paths together.

  b) The sum of the direct relations to any concept is 1.0.

FURTHER QUANTIFICATIONS

You must accept certain necessities when using strength indicators such as the above. In particular you must quantify your measurement techniques and definitions. It is particularly difficult to state a set of hard and fast rules for the quantification of measurement. As Ackoff (1962) has pointed out:

> We can spend an indefinite amount of time trying to specify a set of operations which define measurement. History has shown that such efforts are fruitless, since the operations of measurement are changing and developing progressively as are all other types of scientific operation. . . . We can define [measurement] as a process whose output can be used in a particular way . . . it is a way of obtaining symbols to represent the properties of objects, events, or states, which symbols have the same relevant relationship to each other as do the things which are represented. [p. 179]

The variable being assessed should have its classifications related to each other by the property being measured (e.g., if you are measuring age, persons in the "older" category should have been born before those in the "younger" category).

Different theories need different levels of measurement. If a measurement technique's sole value is to distinguish among two kinds of items (i.e., it acts as an on-off switch), then it can be used only for dichotomous variables. If two or more ordered subconcepts exist, then the classifications composing the associated variable must be ordered, and ordinal statistics must be used for functions.

Different measurements are sensitive to different situations. Rules developed by methodologists for use with certain measurement techniques reflect a theory about how those techniques work. Major disturbing influences should be avoided. For example, the use of white interviewers in black residential areas should be avoided.

RULE 7.5   Proper statement of a measure should include:
   a) what is to be observed;
   b) conditions under which it should be observed;
   c) what measurement operations, if any, should be made;
   d) what instruments and metric are to be used.

RULE 7.6   Describe the capabilities you are demanding of each measure; see to it that the measure fulfills them.

These criteria do not guarantee that your measurements will measure *only* one property and in an appropriate fashion, but they do guarantee that another investigator looking at your results can discern what you did.

Definitions must be quantified simultaneously with measurements. Measurements and definitions are alike in many ways. Both have rules which tell us whether any member of a set belongs also to another set, and these form the basis for quantification. For both to avoid vagueness and contradictions, it is necessary that each object be assigned to one and only one category (in the case of definition, to assign each classification of a variable to one and only one subconcept of the associated concept).

The measurement of a variable and the definition of that same variable in terms of its associated concept should use the same property to order the variable's classifications. Thus the language in which the concept exists must either include a name for the relevant property, or you must invent one. (Many properties of sociological interest are not clearly named in common language.)

If a variable is still unclear, you may be able to order your classifications clearly by using "other" to classify items which do not fall into the specific classifications. You thereby leave one (or possibly several) deliberately ambiguous classification(s). Your measurement goal should be to produce as many perfectly clear, ordered classifications of a variable as possible while still retaining an interesting number of cases in each classification.

RULE 7.7   The measurement and definition of each variable in terms of its associated concept should agree on the property being measured and defined.

Until the last few pages I have limited this book's discussion to *verbal* concepts and *quantified* variables, responding to the fact that, in sociology, ideas are expressed in words and we trust one set of words over another because it corresponds more accurately with the real world. We blurred this clear distinction between words and numbers since, in order to use relations with strength coefficients to indicate a degree of connectedness, your concepts must have a series of subconcepts that are ordered (i.e., if the subconcepts of A are symbolized $a_1, a_2, a_3, \ldots a_n$, you must be able to state for any a_i, that $a_{i+1} > a_i$, or $a_{i+1} < a_i$, etc.). When subconcepts are ordered, definitions can be expressed in terms of equations, such as $v_i = a_i$, or $v_i = a_i + a_{i+1}$. Prediction of specific functions given specific relations can be made with greater precision when you use quantified concepts and variables.

RULE 7.8   When relations include strength as well as sign and direction, quantified definitions are necessary.

MAXIMAL THEORY

Regardless of the kind of theory you are developing, you will be striving to meet maximal as well as minimal criteria. The criteria for maximal theory are: (1) simplicity, (2) completeness, (3) elegance , and (4) uniqueness. Theories hardly ever achieve perfection for any of these criteria, but the combination of emphases that a theorist gives to each plus his methodological sophistication determine his particular theory style.

SIMPLICITY

Simplicity has two aspects: (1) number of premises and (2) complexity. Sociology has so few theories and they cover so little that we sociologists have little to contribute to a discussion of simplicity. Some scientists (including sociologists) believe in simple laws. They follow Whitehead's motto: "A scientist ought to seek simplicity and distrust it." You can seek simplicity by:

1. Picking formulations that are easy to handle;
2. Testing the easier of two theories first;
3. Expressing as many functions as possible through low-order equations (linear, for example).

These judgments are made even though general principles of simplicity have not been formulated and measurement of simplicity seems impossible. Term or concept counting (e.g., one theory has eight concepts whereas another one has six) in a formulation of either mathematical or sentence form does not seem to relate to simplicity. In general, working scientists spend little time worrying about general principles of simplicity; they make intuitive judgments and go on with their work.[1]

As a beginning theorist, you should determine simplicity by comparative judgment. If, after testing your alternatives, you find that the data equally support two or more, select the one that seems simplest to you.

RULE 7.9   Judge simplicity by comparison among alternatives. Trust empirical criteria above all others.

---

[1] Discussion of simplicity paraphrased from Gardner, 1969.

COMPLETENESS

A "complete" theory includes all concepts considered necessary by those working in a field for explanation of a problem in that field. No theory in sociology fulfills this criteria. The most comprehensive sociological theory to date includes fewer than twenty systematically related variables and concepts which (1) have the potential to vary independently and (2) retain significant conceptual status. As a result, sociologists are testing incomplete prototheories and theories, not because they will be fully true, but because they may not be false. Such incomplete theories *may* later form part of a more complete theory.

These incomplete theories are produced by and produce densities (see p. 63) among the collected concepts. The literature generally shows a high density of relations among some concepts and a complete lack of relations elsewhere. These densities focus attention and are also produced by the focused attention of a field.

Completeness and simplicity may be viewed as mirror images of each other, completeness pressing for the widest possible selection of concepts and simplicity for the narrowest. Both are necessary since we consider simple but incomplete theories trivial; and complete but complex ones, unclear and messy. A complete, simple theory would probably have only a few concepts but those would be of a very high order (Chapter 4, pp. 66–67).

RULE 7.10 Judge completeness in your prototheory against the dense segments within the literature.

ELEGANCE

Elegance is a general purpose criterion. When all other factors are equal, you should select one alternative over a second if the first better fulfills the philosophical criteria for theory building. The search for a perfect theory can be overdone. Campbell (1963) points out that those who have mastered the philosophy of science (e.g., Bacon or Carnap) have rarely mastered science, and vice versa.

I will not try to delineate the ideal theory. This is a technical topic in the philosophy of social science just as determination of which statistical technique is suitable to a particular body of data is a technical topic in social science methods and statistics. This chapter's Bibliography suggests further reading in the philosophy of the social sciences.

RULE 7.11   The judgment of elegance is partly a matter of taste and partly a technical matter in the philosophy of science.

UNIQUENESS

Uniqueness is the choice of one theory over another because it attacks a familiar problem in a new way. You must know a problem's history in order to determine uniqueness. A professional contribution to social science must have some unique elements, or it is not a contribution. Articles in professional journals begin with a review of past work so that readers can assess the uniqueness of the new material in the article.

RULE 7.12   Uniqueness must be determined by those who know the preceding literature in an area.

A simple, complete, elegant theory that is also unique is a rare and wonderful event in the history of science. We aim for, but rarely achieve, maximal theories.

CONCLUSIONS

To summarize briefly, we have considered minimal and maximal structural criteria for theory as well as ways to improve the various parts of your prototheory. The sentences (propositions) which make up your prototheory come from a variety of sources; some state complex and contingent theories, others describe experiences, still others provide connecting material. You can translate these into graphs which should have the following properties:

1. For any x and y, where x precedes y in the prototheory, you can write an equation $y = f(x)$.
2. For any data produced for some case, the data can be described by $y = f(x)$.

3. The graph format can be expanded or contracted to meet new theoretical needs.

4. The various parts of the prototheory can be upgraded both structurally and empirically as your skills in theory and research grow.

You have now tested your prototheory empirically and structurally and selected one alternative as a provisional theory. This theory can be a very powerful tool. The following chapters discuss practical uses for your theory.

RULES

RULE 7.1 Remove vagueness from your prototheory by producing two or more clear, alternative statements from that vagueness.

RULE 7.2 Resolve internal contradiction by:
   a) developing alternatives, each of which is internally consistent; *or*
   b) building a more complex model.

RULE 7.3 Resolve contradictory direct and indirect relations by assigning relative strength indicators to relations.

RULE 7.4 *a*) The indirect effect of any concept on any other can be computed by multiplying the indicators along any path and adding separate paths together.
   b) The sum of the direct relations to any concept is 1.0.

RULE 7.5 Proper statement of a measure should include:
   a) what is to be observed;
   b) conditions under which it should be observed;
   c) what measurement operations, if any, should be made;
   d) what instruments and metric are to be used.

RULE 7.6 Describe the capabilities you are demanding of each measure; see to it that the measure fulfills them.

RULE 7.7   The measurement and definition of each variable in terms of its associated concept should agree on the property being measured and defined.

RULE 7.8   When relations include strength as well as sign and direction, quantified definitions are necessary.

RULE 7.9   Judge simplicity by comparison among alternatives. Trust empirical criteria above all others.

RULE 7.10   Judge completeness in your prototheory against the dense segments within the literature.

RULE 7.11   The judgment of elegance is partly a matter of taste and partly a technical matter in the philosophy of science.

RULE 7.12   Uniqueness must be determined by those who know the preceding literature in an area.

EXERCISES

1. Take your prototheory and check it for vagueness. Check definitions and measurement procedures for clarity. For at least two example cases, show how they would be classified into variable classifications and then into subconcepts.
2. Take a prototheory (either the same one as in exercise 1 or another) and check it for internal contradiction. Do this systematically by either listing all pairs and checking one pair of concepts at a time or by using a matrix.
3. Draw a graph including strength indicators (e.g., Figure 7.4 or 7.5) and compute the direct and indirect strength indicators between two pairs of concepts.

BIBLIOGRAPHY

ACKOFF, RUSSELL L. *Scientific Method: Optimizing Applied Research Decisions.* New York: John Wiley & Sons, Inc., 1962.

Ackoff is quite technical and difficult but very much worth reading.

BERGER, P., and T. LUCKMANN. *The Social Construction of Reality*. Garden City, N.Y.: Anchor Books, 1967.
A wordy but interesting discussion of how communities build logics and theories about the world.

BLALOCK, HUBERT. *Theory Construction: From Verbal to Mathematical Formulations*. Englewood Cliffs, N.J.: Prentice-Hall, Inc., 1969.
Section on testing for advanced students.

BUNGE, MARIO. *The Myth of Simplicity: Problems of Scientific Philosophy*. Englewood Cliffs, N.J.: Prentice-Hall, Inc., 1963.
Discussion of simplicity in chapters 4 through 7. The rest of this book is a series of discussions on philosophical problems.

CAMPBELL, NORMAN. *What Is Science?* New York: Dover Publications, Inc., 1952.
A sound and interesting discussion of the philosophy of science in general.

GARDNER, M. "Simplicity As a Scientific Concept: Does Nature Keep Her Accounts on a Thumbnail?" *Scientific American* (Aug. 1969), pp. 118–120.

HUGGINS, W. H., and DORIS R. ENTWISLE. *Introductory Systems and Design*. Waltham, Mass.: Blaisdell Publishing Company, 1968.
A good introduction to general theory of linear systems.

KAPLAN, ABRAHAM. *The Conduct of Inquiry: Methodology for Behavioral Science*. San Francisco: Chandler Publishing Co., 1964.
Less technical than Bunge and more directed to the social sciences. Kaplan makes numerous sensible observations about the structure and organization of theory.

MCCAIN, GARVIN, and ERWIN M. SEGAL. *The Game of Science*. Belmont, Calif.: Brooks/Cole Publishing Co., 1969.
A very simple discussion of the philosophy, psychology, and organization of sicence.

STINCHCOMBE, ARTHUR. *Constructing Social Theories.* New York: Harcourt Brace Jovanovich, Inc., 1968.

Combines a short description of theories (parallel to the one in this book) with a series of theoretical proposals in different areas of sociology. For the advanced student, a good look at a working mind.

ZIMAN, JOHN. *Public Knowledge: The Social Dimension of Science.* Cambridge: Cambridge University Press, 1968.

Ziman emphasizes science as a community built on consensus about what is true.

Chapter 8

PRACTICAL USES OF
THEORY: MODELS

These final three chapters consider such different uses of theory as models, plans, simulations, and games. Their purpose is to suggest how to use theories in the realm of practical decision making. A model (discussed in this chapter) is a device (e.g., a set of mathematical equations) which permits description of the relationships among concepts with sufficient precision to make explanation and prediction exact. A plan (see Chapter 9) is a sequence of events which depend upon one another and whose dependence is predictable either by theory or by "common sense." Simulations and games (the topics of Chapter 10) are similar processes in that both "try out" an aspect of a social situation in isolation from the rest of the world. A simulation emphasizes the relations and interactions of concepts in such situations, and a game, the relations among persons. Certainly each has some aspects of the other. And both can incorporate aspects of plans and models with the result that no clear boundary separates these four, but rather a range of overlap exists among them. Figure 8.1 illustrates the situation.

MODEL SYSTEMS:
   WHY AND HOW
Model systems are best built when you understand the basic on-going processes in a situation and can estimate the effects

Figure 8.1 Games, Simulations, Models, and Plans

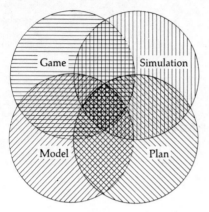

of each process on at least some of the others. Ideally you will arrive at a set of simultaneous equations drawn from your provisional theory (see Chapter 7, pp. 113–115 for linear example).

Population size theory provides an excellent case. We know that the major concepts are "birth," "death," and "migration." We also have estimated variable sizes for these concepts, however crude or unsatisfactory these may be from the data perspective, and a formula for any time period:

$$\text{Change in population size} = \text{birth} - \text{deaths} \\ + \text{inmigration} - \text{outmigration}.$$

Also available for many time periods are numerical estimates for the four variables to the right of the equals sign. If we can fill in those numbers for two points in time with any accuracy, we can compute fairly precisely the change in population size from one time point to the second. Getting those numbers with any accuracy for the same area and the same point in time can be a difficult task, but the accounting logic works by definition whether the numbers are accurate or not.

The above formula is known as the demographic accounting equation. It is not terribly exciting, but it constitutes the

basis for a population growth model. One of the first facts
noted by social scientists studying population growth and
change was that the concept "number of births" in a population depends on the concept "age distribution of the female
population"; if, for example, the total female population is
under 15 or over 45, the model relations will show few births.
Scientists also know that women live longer than men; thus
if women constitute a majority in the population, the model
will show few deaths at young ages.

We can add the concepts "age" and "sex" to this model and
use the diagrammatic form shown in earlier chapters (see Figure 8.2).

Figure 8.2 A Model for Population Size

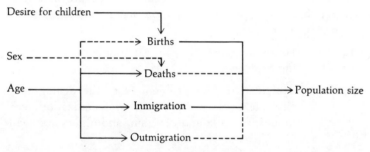

We can improve this model by specifying parts of the
equation. For example, we may find that the present number
of births is some function of the number of female births 15
to 45 years ago. This discovery would suggest a relation
between the concepts "number of births" and "birth rates."
"Birth rate" may also relate to the concept "desire for children" by the female population. Expanding this model and
specifying the components of population size are tasks which
constitute the subject matter of demography as part of social
science in general.

Demographic study has some very practical uses. If we
assume the existence of a world population crisis (i.e., more
children are being born than can be supported by available
space, food, or other resources), someone ought to be making
decisions to relieve the situation. Assuming that the available

models of population growth are perfectly reasonable, what kinds of decisions can we make?

PROBLEM SOLVING

Let us step back for a moment and consider problem solving in general. I have assumed that most readers will not become professional sociologists and that your interests in social analysis are partly intellectual and partly practical. For example, if the world population becomes 430 billion people by 2030, an intensely practical problem will exist (the present population is only 3 billion and many people even now are improperly fed). You do not have the time, energy, information, or technical expertise to analyze such a problem fully, but you can make a start. The general steps are invariably clearer than their application to a particular problem, but the following is a beginning:

RULE 8.1 Formulate your problem (e.g., population is increasing explosively).

RULE 8.2 Systematize your problem (e.g., the demographic example uses two different systematization techniques, formula and diagram, and others are available).

TIME. Your planning time is that time which exists between your recognition that a specific decision is needed and the time when that decision (or set of decisions) is actually made. When a rock is flying at your head, you are given only reflex time; most other decisions offer potentially longer planning times. Your energy for analysis depends on the number of alternative demands being simultaneously made on you or on the group that is planning; you must be able to rank demands so that you spend your planning time on those concerns that are most important to you.

Planning time for the demographic example was set during 1952–1954 when the United Nations first made world population estimates and projections, and demographers became aware of the total human population size and its growth potential (Bogue, 1969).

INFORMATION. You need two kinds of planning information: (1) a prototheory or theory about the world affecting your problem, and (2) the facts of your specific case. The preceding chapters showed you how to develop a working prototheory into a testable form. If you work without explicit theory, you risk using not only an incomplete but possibly an inconsistent theory to make decisions.

For the population case, the gathering of accurate information on present population size, age and sex distribution, fertility rates, and changes in these factors over time constitutes a major difficulty. For the nonprofessional, professional reports such as the UN data are quite adequate.

RULE 8.3 Gather information about your problem and possible solutions during your planning time.

Given planning time and information, you can begin proposing alternative solutions to your problem. If you can find only one solution, systematize it (solutions as well as problems need systematization) and carry it out; you have no need to look further.

RULE 8.4 After your initial study, determine your alternative solutions; propose at least two alternative routes to solving your problem (if neither you nor anyone else can see more than one solution, you have no problem).

One way to generate solutions is to examine the variables included in your systematization of the problem.

SOLUTIONS: MANIPULATABLE VARIABLES

Let us begin by considering only those concept-variable units within alternatives that both precede and affect your prototheory's goal. In examining these we will find that given (1) a specific length of time for which to plan, (2) a certain point in history when that planned-for period will occur, and (3) your particular social position, you can change the values of some variables in the units you are considering by altering your use of available time, resources, commitment, and personnel. In this way "manipulatable" variables can focus your planning. For example, if we consider the theory proposed in Figure 8.2, the two source concepts are age and sex. These factors in a given population will change only if given a fairly long period of time. If the theory were modified as in Figure 8.3, however, we might have two manipulatable variables: (1) the population control program and (2) the desirability of an area for inmigration.

Figure 8.3 A More Complete Model for Population Size

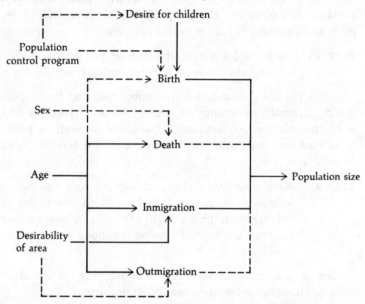

These concepts can be manipulated by some person(s), but you may not be that someone. Practically speaking, you usually want to find those concepts on which *you* can have some effect. In actual planning situations, you may find your prototheory too crude to use because *you* can only change some variables by amounts too small to be measured in the gross terms which we have been considering.

Your ultimate ability to manipulate population size conceptually and actually depends on how strongly connected (1) the population control program is to the birth rate and (2) the birth rate is to the population size (we know, for example, that for industrial societies, birth rate is the *most* important determinant of size).

If your goal appears unaffected by any variable that you can manipulate, you might investigate whether a more complete theory of any of the major causal variables might not provide a tool for manipulation. If this avenue proves fruitless, consider the various factors to which your goal might be sensitive and at least keep track of these. Individual cases are rarely so clear-cut that you either can or cannot affect your goal. Usually you are monitoring several major causes of a goal and working very hard to produce small changes in the direction you prefer.

Your prototheory can help you allocate your resources if you can (1) determine which variables are manipulatable and (2) assign cost figures to each. Cost may be in money, time, or any other comparable quantity (influence, equipment, wear, etc.). If alternate means to your goal exist, the costs of each can be compared. You need to know how much change in each variable is necessary to produce a change in subsequent variables before you can determine the various costs accurately, but this information may well be readily available to you.

RULE 8.5 Identify those concept-variable units in your prototheory on which you can have an effect. Estimate (1) the length of time necessary to effect desired changes and (2) how large those changes will be.

SOLUTIONS: OTHER VARIABLES

Only some of the variables affecting the conclusion we want to reach are manipulatable by us to any degree. Some may be influenced by us and some by others. And some concept-variable units (e.g., "age" and "sex" in the demographic example), at least within the bounds of the theories we have, are just plain intractable to anyone at all. These variables, for the purposes of practical theory, are simply "given." They may change but only as a response to circumstances beyond our control. Yet clearly these variables have an effect, sometimes a controlling effect, on the outcomes we want to reach.

You can take three courses of action with these variables: *predict, monitor*, and/or *research* them. Predicting the course of events is a very old idea; seers and fortune tellers have always done a good business. Asymmetric theory has a time order, so you *can* predict that the values of "later" variables will be those that would be appropriate, given the known preceding variables. Take the Berelson and Steiner material, for example, and assume that it takes one year for a crisis to effect decentralization and another year for decentralization to change communication; if you know that an organization is experiencing a crisis now, you can predict that, two years from now, communication will be low.

Or you can predict the unknown values of variables even as they are happening. Again consider the Berelson material. You have no information on tolerance, but you do know the decentralization rating; from this information you can predict the degree of tolerance you would find if you were to look for it.

You can also monitor intractable variables so that changes in them do not catch you by surprise. Almost anything can be monitored, given that you (1) know what you are looking for and (2) spend enough time, energy, and resources. Such monitoring may allow you to predict the short-run future values of these variables.

The third approach, if you care enough and have resources for the task, is research into the causes of these variables. Some way may conceivably exist to modify even the most intractable variable. Research into weather modification often seems completely hopeless because the forces involved are enormous and we lack comparable sources of force, yet some small progress in modification has been made.

To summarize then:

RULE 8.6   For variables over which you have no control, (1) predict their future levels, (2) monitor the important ones, and/or (3) do research for better predictors and possible tools for manipulation.

IMPLEMENTATION

If you have at least one solution which incorporates a manipulatable variable, you will want to develop and implement a plan to affect the value of that variable.

Actual implementation of your plan will probably involve a series of sequence plans (see Chapter 9). Such plans involve careful planning of the use of your resources and the timing of that use.

Implementation itself can happen in two ways. Usually and unfortunately, you may have to implement your plan all at once and in all places or parts of a system at once. If you can, you should test your theory and the plans derived from it in an experimental situation and evaluate the results (see below for discussion of this procedure). One example of implementation is the spread of family planning clinics and programs to practically every country in the world. Once the world's population potential was recognized, efforts to control population size began.

The practical situation within which you must work may make your planning situation intellectually difficult. The government and many other large organizations can afford to implement reasonably sloppy planning because, as powerful organizations, they can simply push aside many mistakes and operate at less than optimum levels. In addition, because they have substantial resources, their planning is generally quite elegant but limited in scope to a few variables. They can afford this luxury because they control the most important change factors for many of the items in which they are interested. By contrast the techniques I am suggesting are not limited in their usefulness or validity to such powerful entities, either present or future.

RULE 8.7 Implement your plan.

EVALUATION PROCEDURES[1]

Practical theories need testing that reveals how a specific theory's goals are being achieved. Testing should also indicate

---

[1] Discussion in this section based on Suchman (1967).

why some programs or parts of plans succeed and others fail. The practical operation of a plan requires that you design evaluation procedures simultaneously with the plan itself.

DESIGN. In designing an evaluation procedure, you must first establish a goal or goals for the plan being evaluated. What is the *content* of that goal?

1. To change a level of knowledge?
2. To alter attitudes and/or behaviors?
3. To expose someone to something?
4. To promote awareness and interest?
5. To cause action?
6. What magnitude of effect is sought?

You must also know *who* will be affected by the program. (In the infelicitous phrase of planners, who is the "target population"?) and *when* is the change to occur?

After the content, population, and time questions have been answered, you can ask what kinds of data will assist evaluation and how each goal being evaluated will relate to that data. And before determining specific information, you need to know what problems can be expected with the project. For example, if the project is subject to political pressure, then you must assess that factor as well as the project's activity. And you will also need a procedural definition of project activity that is measurable.

DATA AND TESTING. You can gather two fundamentally different kinds of data about projects: opinions and records. Each can be taken from either the "target" population or the plan's executors. Table 8.1 shows both kinds of data matched with both information sources. Which route you choose depends on what you want to know. If results, either potential or as a matter of past history, are your major concern, you will check public opinion and information in public records. If you would rather know what an organization is doing, regardless of the effect it is having, you will prefer the planner's information.

Table 8.1   Types of Evaluation Data

Source of Data	Opinions	Records
Target population	Public opinion survey	Diaries Any bookkeeping project Newspapers by target population
Planners	Interviews with personnel	Time records Money records

RULE 8.8   Evaluate your implementation using the following steps:

- *a)* Determine the goals to be assessed.
- *b)* Determine the content and size of change desired.
- *c)* Identify the affected population.
- *d)* Assess specific problems with the project.
- *e)* Determine the means you will use for producing change, describe it, and standardize the description.
- *f)* Select the kind of information you need.

In evaluating a plan, you will want to establish criteria that parallel the plan's objectives. In addition to effort and effect as perceived by the target population and planners, you might also want to assess:

1. Adequacy of each participant's performance in light of need and resources;
2. Efficiency in terms of the alternatives available;
3. Why the plan is working as it is. Analyze the population, situation, and different effects of the program.

You should do further research to reassess intermediate goals as well as means. If your information on needs is good, you can evaluate the adequacy of a project in filling those needs. If you have a series of alternative proposals, you can ask about relative efficiency in need fulfillment.

The questioning of "workability" suggests the existence of a prior theory as to why the plan might work. Evaluation requires that you find (or not find) evidence that the changes observed result from the plan employed to bring them about. You should note the existence of preconditions, some of which affect your plan and some of which do not; of intervening variables, some affected and others not; and of consequences, some affected by any of the above and others not. Diagrammatically, the situation is that shown in Figure 8.4.

Figure 8.4 The Evaluation Situation

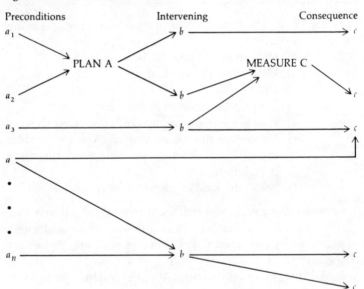

You can measure some of your variables (marked a, b, c) and determine results, but unless you have a *control group* matched to your experiment group, you will have no way to discern whether the degree of change occurring has resulted directly from project activities or from other sources. Therefore:

RULE 8.9 Establish a control group for testing programs or plans.

Testing of this nature questions the deepest theoretical basis for one's activities. Suggestions which might make testing more useful include: (1) avoid conceptualizing a model solely within one discipline; the complexity of a real situation exceeds the limits of any small, abstract model; (2) assure public access to the whole operation; a model case for public access is the agricultural experiment station.

Experiments can and have gone wild. If an experiment is set up by people who believe in it (as is almost always the case), and if they are persuasive, they may not wait until analysis is done before trying to move to large-scale implementations. Moynihan's discussion of community action programs in *Maximum Feasible Misunderstanding* indicates what the results of such precipitous action can be.

RULE 8.10 *a*) Use concepts from more than one discipline.

   b) Assure public access to the entire operation.

MODEL USE

The necessity of a clear model for adequate planning should be very evident from the above discussion. You begin with a prototheory composed of the major concept-variable units necessary to understand a particular situation; you next test and work that prototheory into a provisional theory usable on your problem. You are now ready to ask: "What can I do to assure that certain variables in the real situation will have certain values or ranges of values at some point in the future?" For some situations plans may be useful. But if your problem involves either allocation or inventory problems, you will probably find models more helpful.

ALLOCATION PROBLEMS

Resources need to be distributed, and you have some measure of return for alternative uses.

EXAMPLE 1. Birth control devices for a population. You have shipments coming to Area X, and you must make choices about their distribution.

EXAMPLE 2. Time allocation. Your schedule for a day includes 24 hours and you have activities for 26 hours, not including sleep.

INVENTORY PROBLEMS

You have the capacity to produce and store a "product" for which a variable demand exists. Production and storage costs are known. You want to know how much to produce and store.

EXAMPLE 1. Ph.D. holders have been stored in "soft money" (research) jobs until permanent positions become available. Now "soft money" jobs are becoming scarce; the demand for permanent teachers with Ph.D.'s is also changing.

EXAMPLE 2. You need to know the costs of making friends now versus the costs of doing so later and not having to maintain those friendships during the interim. You should include the loss factor to you from the *lack* of friendship over the time between "now" and "later."

PROBLEMS INAPPROPRIATE TO MODEL PLANNING

There are problems for which model planning is *not* appropriate.

EXAMPLE 1. A search problem. What kinds of information will you need in order to make a rational decision about a problem? Such questions relate to the quality of your theory about a given problem because, if you know how things fit together, you should be able to determine what data you will need to predict outcomes. Search questions are very difficult when you know that your theory is not quite right and your available data somewhat inaccurate.

EXAMPLE 2. Organizational structure. How can you best plan channels of communication, authority, and resource flow to produce any of several ends? Organizational structure questions present two interacting difficulties. First, we lack good techniques for analyzing organizational structure. Second, we know that many objectives are included in the choice of one organizational structure over another, but the relation of those objectives to particular structures has not been worked out in any form that would facilitate combining several objectives at once. Decisions about structure, then, are normally made on the basis of some, not necessarily rational, "rule of thumb" (e.g., how many people a man can supervise) or political necessity.

These examples remind us that many important and interesting questions do not lend themselves to solution through model construction.

Chapter 9 discusses a second use for theory, sequence planning.

RULES

RULE 8.1   Formulate your problem (e.g., population is increasing explosively).

RULE 8.2   Systematize your problem (e.g., the demographic example uses two different systematization techniques, formula and diagram, and others are available).

RULE 8.3   Gather information about your problem and possible solutions during your planning time.

RULE 8.4   After your initial study, determine your alternative solutions; propose at least two alternative routes to solving your problem (if neither you nor anyone else can see more than one solution, you have no problem).

RULE 8.5   Identify those concept-variable units in your proto-theory on which you can have an effect. Estimate (1) the length of time necessary to effect desired changes and (2) how large those changes will be.

RULE 8.6   For variables over which you have no control, (1) predict their future levels, (2) monitor the important ones, and/or (3) do research for better predictors and possible tools for manipulation.

RULE 8.7   Implement your plan.

RULE 8.8 Evaluate your implementation using the following steps:

    a) Determine the goals to be assessed.

    b) Determine the content and size of change desired.

    c) Identify the affected population.

    d) Assess specific problems with the project.

    e) Determine the means you will use for producing change, describe it, and standardize the description.

    f) Select the kind of information you need.

RULE 8.9 Establish a control group for testing programs or plans.

RULE 8.10   *a*) Use concepts from more than one discipline.

    b) Assure public access to the entire operation.

EXERCISES

1. Choose a problem.
    a) Pick a goal.
    b) Describe at least five nonmanipulatable and four manipulatable concepts and associated variables that will affect your outcome.
    c) State the relationships you believe to hold among the concepts. Cite sources for any which have been tested or observed.
    d) Order the variables using a graph.
2. Set up a plan to change the value of one variable you have described above.
3. Design an evaluation procedure for the plan.

BIBLIOGRAPHY

ACKOFF, RUSSELL L., and MAURICE SASIENI. *Fundamentals of Operations Research*. New York: John Wiley & Sons, Inc., 1968.

    A very good technical summary of what we know about decision making.

BOGUE, DONALD J. *Principles of Demography*. New York: John Wiley & Sons, Inc., 1969.

Bogue presents the population control problem in an interesting and controversial manner. The precision necessary to demographic statements results in a very long book, however.

FORRESTER, JAY W. *Urban Dynamics*. Cambridge, Mass.: The MIT Press, 1969.

Another system model, in this case a city. Forrester's model lacks much empirical foundation, but it provides a very good introduction to thinking about a whole social system.

MOYNIHAN, DANIEL P. *Maximum Feasible Misunderstanding*. New York: The Free Press, 1969.

A description of how to make hash of a good idea by implementing it everywhere, all at once.

SUCHMAN, E. *Evaluative Research*. New York: Russell Sage Foundation, 1967.

A good discussion of evalaution. This book is the basis for the discussion of evaluation in this chapter.

PRACTICAL USES OF THEORY: SEQUENCE PLANNING

If you need to plan an event that falls into, or can be made analogous to, one of the following categories of problems, then you have a sequence planning problem:

1. The routing of men, supplies, and so on, through a system which includes a set of tasks to be accomplished and few processors to do them (called queueing if the problem is to minimize the length of a processing line);

2. The planning of a series of activities that must occur in a certain order, or in which some activities must occur before others;

3. The coordination of a series of activities so that they are completed within a minimum time period;

4. A series of decisions that must be made in an orderly fashion.

Each of these problems can be initially approached through a very simple structure which will be laid out on the following pages. What I propose is a method for allocating priorities to individual jobs so that they can be done in the most effective order.

You might wonder why I have included sequence planning. Theories are, after all, about attributes rather than events, and sequence plans are about events and series of events. So let us take an example. If you have a theory about elections in which the candidate's popularity appears as a concept (as it clearly should), and if you want to have someone elected, your prototheory may not tell you what specific concepts relate to "popularity." As a matter of fact, scanning all the available sources, you see nothing which usefully tells you what concepts relate to popularity, except perhaps "increased exposure," and even exposure can have ambiguous effects. You probably do know, however, that an event like a rally can increase exposure and perhaps popularity. So you decide to have a rally.

Because we often work from crude theory and with such unhelpful variables when we are planning something specific, we must resort to sequence planning until we know the facts required for good model planning.

PROCESS

Let us begin with an idea for a plan to test this theory about political campaigns and a candidate's popularity. You have conceptualized that increased exposure relates to increased popularity. To test this relation you want to expose the candidate through rallies, testimonial dinners, and the like. The plan should include not only the completed activity but all of the individual activities that must be finished before the final event can be completed. Many of these activities will be interdependent. Therefore, to produce a result in some reasonable time without duplication of effort, you must order your efforts on the activities. The necessity for a particular order may exist because the theory indicates more effect from one order than another, or because experience indicates that item one must be completed before item two. A sequence should not be set either by resources or by preexisting patterns.

Diagram symbolization, using arrows, is very helpful in picturing sequences. The initial symbolization of plans for a political rally could look like Fig. 9.1. You draw an arrow on the basis that the first event must be completed before the

Figure 9.1 Plan: Step 1

Start ― ― ― ― ― ― ― ― ― ―→Political rally

second. If no arrow connects two items, then no relation exists between them and they can proceed simultaneously or in any order.

As you begin planning the rally in more detail, you will find that people, a place, and a speaker will be needed. These needs can be symbolized as in Figure 9.2. Although practical

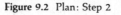

Figure 9.2 Plan: Step 2

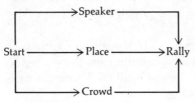

experience would indicate that neither the speaker, the place, nor the crowd must necessarily precede the other two items, all three should probably be available by rally time (a conclusion which some would question). Any of the items in Figure 9.2 could remain unplanned. You might bring off a spontaneous demonstration, for example, by planning only for a speaker and a small crowd to "start the ball rolling," leaving the place undecided in the expectation that these ingredients will gradually attract a large crowd. Other examples exist, but let us develop, as practice, a plan for a full-blown, standard political rally designed to aid a campaign for public office. A detailed rally plan might look like Figure 9.5; the basic set of necessities for a rally, however, would look like Figure 9.2. Now you can begin expanding 9.2 into a complete plan.

The first step is to consider the top branch (speaker) of Figure 9.2 in detail. You must select, contact, and confirm a main speaker. Some considerations determine whom to select (e.g., should you get a "name" speaker because you need a large turnout?). Once confirmed, whom will he draw? Is he a party wheelhorse who will bring out only the party faithful? (The answer to this question will affect the crowd-drawing plans.) Does he have any enemies (or friends) among local persons? Who should be invited? Does the speaker use visual aids, including cue cards? What should the remainder of the program include? At this point, consider the branches you are proposing (see Figure 9.3).

Figure 9.3 Plan: Step 3

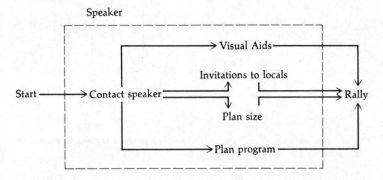

Now examine "visual aids" in more detail. If the speaker uses visual aids, or if, as part of the planned program, you intend to use a national TV hookup (perhaps a major party figure is going to address the meeting on a big screen, etc.), you will need to employ someone who can handle these matters. You should probably ask for cost estimates and sign a contract with the company giving the lowest bid. If the speaker uses cue cards, you will have to make them, after first obtaining a copy of his text for this purpose (see Figure 9.4). As long as you have a copy of the speech, you might produce prespeech copies of it for the press and distribute them just before speech time so that quotes will be accurate and stories will make the 11:00 P.M. news broadcasts.

Although it will still not be complete, you can easily generate a full plan such as Figure 9.5 from such thinking. With each planning problem you move back and forth across the figure, always asking, "What is necessary before I can do this?" and "Where does this step lead?" Drawing such a network can be a rewarding occupation in itself because it forces you to work through a plan in detail. You thereby increase your probability of catching oversights and finding

Figure 9.4 Plan: Step 4

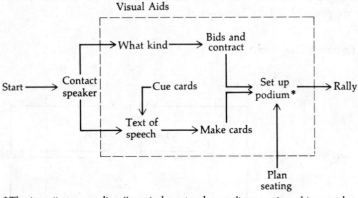

*The item "set up podium" reminds us to plan podium seating; this must be done before set-up time.

new tasks (e.g., podium seating plans), previously not part of your thinking, which need to be accomplished. A diagram can help you coordinate many people effectively.

The real value of this technique is not realized, however, until you have made some simple calculations with respect to your plan. These calculations require a systematic numbering of the plan's parts. Every job's number must be larger than all jobs that precede it and smaller than all that follow it in the sequence. You should leave some gaps for additions and re-numbering. The numbers on Figure 9.5 represent such calculations.

After numbering your diagram you should note (1) the length of time each job will take, (2) the time scheduled for each job, and (3) the amount of leeway left in the total project and at various points.

To do this job in detail you should design a table like Table 9.1, which lists all jobs with the length of time and number of men each requires. Here you must estimate (based on experience or advice), and you may be wrong. You may want to note on the diagram those estimates that are the most shaky. A prototheory with time parameters will help in this task.

Figure 9.5 Complete Plan with Event Numbers

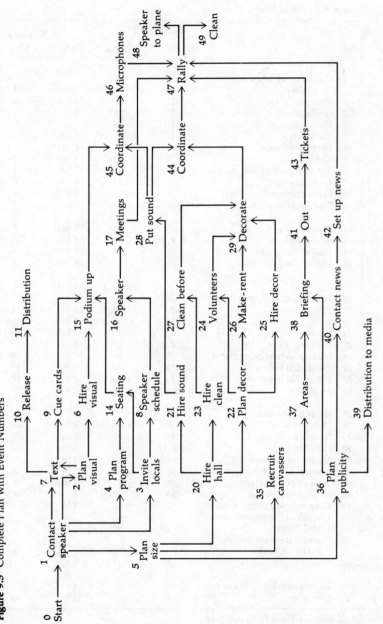

Table 9.1 Time Plan

Job		Performed Before	Performed After	Time	Number of Men
0	Start	—	1	—	—
1	Contact and schedule speaker	0	2, 3, 4, 5, 7	1 mo	1
2	Plan visual aids	1	6, 7	4 hrs	2
3	Invite locals	1	8, 14	8 hrs	4
4	Plan program	1	14	6 hrs	2
5	Plan size	1	20, 35, 36	1 hr	1
6	Hire visual aids	2	15	8 hrs	1
7	Get text	1, 2	9, 10	4 hrs	1
8	Set up meetings and photos	3	16	12 hrs	3
9	Make cue cards	7	15	8 hrs	2
10	Press prespeech copies	7	11	8 hrs	4
11	Distribute to press	10	—	1 hr	2
*					
14	Plan seating	3, 4	15	8 hrs	3
15	Set up podium	6, 9, 14	45	4 hrs	12
16	Pick up speaker	8	17	1 hr	1
17	Make scheduled stops	16	47	8 hrs	1
*					
20	Hire hall	5	21, 22, 23	4 hrs	1
21	Hire sound company	20	28	4 hrs	1
22	Plan decor	20	24, 25, 26	10 hrs	3
23	Contract cleaning	20	27	8 hrs	1
24	Recruit	22	29	8 hrs	10
25	Hire decorator	22	29	2 hrs	3
26	Make and rent decorations	22	29	30 hrs	10
27	Clean hall before	23	29	6 hrs	40
28	Place loud speakers	21	44, 45	8 hrs	10
29	Decorate	24, 25, 26, 27	44	6 hrs	100
*					
35	Recruit canvassers	5	37	8 hrs	10
36	Plan publicity	5	28, 29, 40	4 hrs	3
37	Divide areas	35	38	1 hr	1
38	Give briefing	36, 37	41	2 hrs	3
39	Media distribution	36	—	10 hrs	10
40	Contact news departments	36	42	2 hrs	2
41	Send out canvassers	38	43	48 hrs	4
42	News setup in hall	40	47	14 hrs	10
43	Give tickets to canvassers	41	47	1 hr	5
44	Coordinate loudspeakers and decor	28, 29	47	2 hrs	3
45	Coordinate loudspeaker system & podium	15, 28	46	2 hrs	3
46	Adjust microphones	45	47	1 hr	1
47	Rally	17, 43, 44, 46	48, 49	3 hrs	—
48	Return speaker to plane	47	—	1 hr	1
49	Clean up	47	—	30 hrs	40

* Allowance for additional tasks.

Since this kind of planning requires counting back from a specific time rather than beginning at a specific time, you should figure the available "leeway" backwards from the end time to the beginning. To use a part of this time planning as an example, you work backwards from job 29, giving it an arbitrary beginning time of —8 hours (8 hours before the rally), you can assign the necessary starting times to all jobs that must be completed by the time 29 is begun by subtracting the time it takes to do the job from the starting time for 29. Some of this planning is done in Table 9.2.

Table 9.2 Examples of Leeway Computation

Job	Length	Men	Latest Start Time	Leeway
20	4	1	—52	—*
21	4	1	—15	33
22	10	3	—48	0
23	8	1	—22	26
24	8	10	—16	22
25	2	1	—10	28
26	30	10	—38	0
27	6	40	—14	0
29	6	100	— 8	0

* Not defined since 20 is the first job in *this* sequence.

Consider also how you compute the starting time of job 22 in this sequence. This task must be completed *before* any of the jobs dependent on it can be started. You must find the earliest starting time among the jobs depending on 22 (in this case the —38 of job 26) and subtract the length of job 22 from (—38), which tells you that job 22 must start at —48. At this point you make an interesting discovery. If job 22 is completed at time —38 and job 24 need not start until —16, you have gained 22 hours of free time for job 24 during which time you can either (1) let job 24 slide, (2) start it with fewer men and spread it out, or (3) complete it early and proceed to the next job if all preliminaries to that job have been finished. Job 24 is an 8-hour job for 10 men; it might be a 16-hour job for 5 men. You might experiment to see whether fewer men working longer can do the job. This either releases men to work elsewhere or removes the necessity to hire or recruit them in the first place.

Figure 9.6 is the completed diagram for Figure 9.5 with starting times and leeway computed. Note the string 1, 5, 35,

Figure 9.6 Plan with Event Numbers and Amount of Leeway

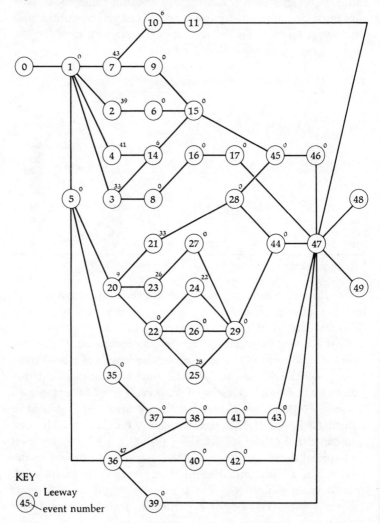

KEY

Leeway

event number

37, 38, 41, 43, 47. This string has no leeway at all. It is called the "Critical Path" for this project. In managing this project, you must watch completion times and work loads along this path very carefully so as not to slow down the whole operation. Maybe more canvassers would cut down the time on job 41.

By manipulating the use of resources and analyzing the effect of each manipulation on the outcome, you can arrive at an optimal plan for utilization of your resources to produce the rally in the amount of time available to you. These diagrams constitute the beginnings of a series of techniques which advanced students may want to examine further. These include:

1. Critical Path techniques, which emphasize the reduction of time required to produce a planned activity;

2. PERT (Project Evaluation and Review Technique), which emphasizes occurrence time and scheduling;

3. PPBS (Plans and Program Budgeting System), which emphasizes the cost of alternative paths to the same results.

This chapter's Bibliography contains references to several good sources. Instead of summarizing rules for this total procedure, I will give just one general rule:

RULE 9.1   Use sequence planning to order a series of events.

DECISION TREES

Other planning techniques are also available. One is a decision tree, often used when there are a limited number of alternatives, each leading either to other decisions or to some variety of response from the environment (either human or otherwise). Decision trees can be very useful in determining which of a series of items to use in a sequence planning situation.

Suppose you are trying to decide what to have for dessert from the choices offered on a restaurant's dessert list (pie, cake, ice cream). If you decide to eat pie, you will want to know what kinds of pie are available. As you go through the selection process, you begin to unfold a decision tree. A full decision tree regarding dessert might look like Figure 9.7. A decision tree lays out all of your alternative decisions and orders the sequence in which decisions must be made. Like sequence diagrams the exercise of laying out alternatives is useful in itself, and with a little computation we can again come to some interesting and even more useful conclusions.

Figure 9.7   A Dessert Decision Tree

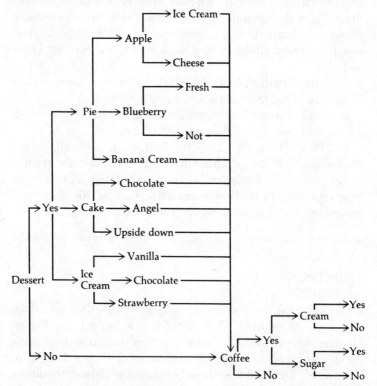

For example, you want to decide whether to repair a car yourself or to let a shop do it. The shop has estimated $40 to repair one problem and $60 to do a second. You can repair the more expensive of the two yourself in 10 hours and the less expensive in another 10. (The car is still running, but if either problem becomes much worse, the car will stop.) You also have an estimate from the repair shop of the likelihood that the problems will worsen, and you can guess how your repairs would compare with shop repairs.

A decision tree for this example would look like Figure 9.8. You read the tree as follows. If the shop repairs both problems (alternative A), there is a .9 chance that the jobs will be

Figure 9.8 Car Repair Decisions

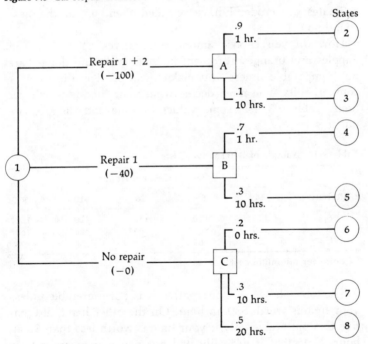

correctly done, and you will have spent time only in taking the car to and from the shop. If you choose alternative B, there is a .7 probability that you will have to spend time only taking the car to the shop but a .3 probability that the car will break down and you will need to spend 10 hours fixing it. Decisions that you must make are symbolized with circles, and environment decisions (any decisions made not by you but by others or by nature) with squares. Also shown are the costs of each alternative and the probabilities for environment decisions.

To evaluate this diagram multiply the chance times the cost of each alternative and add those that result from the same decision. So for alternative A, multiply .9 times 1 hour and .1 times 10 hours and add. This gives a cost total of 1.9 hours and $100 for making that decision. (Since the time estimates are crude, I have rounded them up to the next round hour.)

How do you choose among alternatives? You have an "apples and oranges" problem in that hours and dollars are not comparable unless you make them so. For the sake of comparability, you must decide what your time is worth per hour. Table 9.3 lists some values of time and their consequences.

Table 9.3   Example of Alternative Costs

Alternative	Cost per Hour				
	$4	$5	$6	$10	$30
A	108	110	112	120	160*
B	56	60*	64*	80*	160*
C	52*	65	78	130	390

* Choice for minimum cost.

The table shows that alternative A is not preferable unless your time is worth $30 an hour. On the other hand, alternative C is preferable only if your time is worth less than $5 an hour. Note that it probably will not pay you to make finer distinctions than this. You could, for example, solve the three simultaneous equations for optimum values, but what difference would this make? More advanced students may want to apply linear programming techniques.

RULE 9.2   Use decision trees to help you select appropriate sequences.

CONCLUSION

To summarize, you have just read through one graphic technique for sequencing events and one for selecting appropriate sequences. These techniques will help you plan activities by outlining what needs to be done, when, and in what order. They also identify and highlight potential problems. You should be aware that techniques such as these are only as good as the research, experience, and understanding that go into them; you need not necessarily be impressed by a "classy" diagram.

Chapter 10 discusses simulations and games, two more practical uses for theory.

RULES

RULE 9.1   Use sequence planning to order a series of events.

RULE 9.2   Use decision trees to help you select appropriate sequences.

EXERCISES

1. Select a goal and describe a strategy for achieving this goal.
    a) Specify a rough time table:
        (1) beginning date
        (2) ten major events or actions (be specific) and sequences
        (3) end date
    b) What chances for success have you? Be specific about five major factors leading to success and five leading to failure.
    c) What chance is there that someone will try your plan?
2. Use a decision tree to lay out the alternatives for some real decision: Evaluate the tree and indicate what you decide.
3. Evaluate a plan.
    a) Get the facts.
        (1) What was your part in the operation? What did

you see and hear? A diary report is appropriate, but a postmortem format can be used.

(2) Did the agents of the plan carry out their parts correctly? If not, why not?

(3) How accurate was the plan (1) in timing, (2) in assigning outcomes to different activities, and (3) in assessing opposition?

b) Assess present situation.

(1) What is the present situation and can you tell if the alternatives proposed in your prototheory are appropriate?

    (a) If not, is reassessment of the whole plan in order, and how would you begin?

    (b) If yes, what are those alternatives and which do you propose to follow?

(2) On balance, are you closer to the goal than you were?

c) Further planning.

(1) Is there more that you should know?

(2) What will be the basis of alternate plans?

BIBLIOGRAPHY

BATTERSBY, ALBERT. *Mathematics in Management.* Baltimore, Md.: Penguin Books, 1966.

Simple techniques of rational planning with examples and principles clearly explained.

EWING, DAVID W. *The Practice of Planning.* New York: Harper & Row, 1968.

Sections on Critical Path analysis and decision trees are applicable.

FAIRWEATHER, GEORGE. *Methods for Experimental Social Innovation.* New York: John Wiley & Sons, Inc., 1967.

Discussion of how to plan change.

KAHN, ALFRED J. *Studies in Social Policy and Planning.* New York: Russell Sage Foundation, 1969.

Contains case histories of social planning.

KAHN, ALFRED J. *Theory and Practice of Social Planning.* New York: Russell Sage Foundation, 1969.

A detailed examination of social planning. This volume discusses the process of planning.

PRACTICAL USES OF THEORY: SIMULATIONS AND GAMES

We use simulations and games to develop and test theories. They aid development as a source of concepts, and they can test the internal consistency and effects of relation patterns in concept sets when real social situations are too important, too large, extended over too long a period of time, too uncertain, or too inaccessible in time or space to permit other tests. We game nuclear war, for example, not because we think it is fun but because we have only one earth and the possible consequences are too great to risk experimentation.

The differences between simulation and gaming are not clear-cut. In a simulation, emphasis is on the relation between the inputs and the outcomes of a process. A simulation may be a set of differential equations into which varying inputs can be channeled and resulting outcomes compared. A simulation uses a model or plan (such as are developed in Chapters 8 and 9) and then tests that model or plan for possible outcomes given certain sets of inputs. A game must involve inputs of skill, knowledge, or just activity from at least one human or quasi-human player. Dice games, which require little skill at the game per se (although substantial skill at the psychology of betting), and chess games played by computers are clearly marginal "games" by this definition.

In a game, the person(s) involved can affect the outcome of the game by a single decision or action. Simulation and gaming both provide opportunities for predicting, confirming an explanation, testing the internal reliability of a theory, and checking the assumptions of policy changes.

Computer development has made simulation and gaming much easier and more common. Computers can do the bookkeeping for a complex game, provide a neutral (sometimes random) input source for games, or run hundreds of time periods in a simulation easily. This ease has attracted much attention to these techniques within the social sciences.

SIMULATIONS

A simulation normally uses a model or plan and examines the outcome of that model or plan when the values of certain variables are fixed at one level while others are changed. Usually, but not necessarily, the *fixed variables* are those that we earlier considered nonmanipulatable. The variables that are changed (*control variables*) are those considered manipulatable. The interest is largely in those effects (*output variables*) that will occur after several time periods.

For example, if you were appointed to start a new college and wanted to know the number of students to expect each fall so that you could supply enough housing, instructors, and so on, a student population simulation might be useful. In such a simulation the major processes are the input of freshmen every September and the exit of graduating seniors every June. Minor processes that add students include the acceptance of transfers, the addition of special students, and the return of former students. Minor processes that subtract include college termination, transfers out, temporary dropouts, and death.

If you know the attrition rates for each class, the number of entering freshmen, and the number and timing of small additions and subtractions, you can simulate with some confidence the number of students on campus at any time, the number in each class, and the number of graduating seniors. Let us develop the example by assuming that your new college will admit 800 freshmen and that you know the total attrition rates for each class (see Table 10.1).

Table 10.1 Simulation of a College Population

	No. of Students in Sept.	Attrition (%)	No. of Students in June
Year 1			
Freshmen	800	20	640
Total	800	20	640
Year 2			
Freshmen	800		640
Sophomores	640	10	576
Total	1440		1216
Year 3			
Freshmen	800	20	640
Sophomores	640	10	576
Juniors	576	08	530
Total	2016		1746
Year 4			
Freshmen	800	20	640
Sophomores	640	10	576
Juniors	576	08	530
Seniors	530	10	477
Total	2546		2223

In year 1 you admit the 800 freshmen for a total of 800 students on campus (the number admitted is a *control variable*). There is a 20 percent attrition rate between September and June for freshmen (the attrition rate is a *fixed variable*); thus June finds the college with 640 freshmen left. In September of year 2, you again admit 800 freshmen for a total of 1440 students on campus; with 20 percent freshmen and 10 percent sophomore attrition rates, you have 1216 students left in June (1216 is an *intermediate value*). By year 4, the total population is 2546 in September and 2223 in June. You graduate exactly 477 seniors. If these processes are exactly stable, then the population will remain at the level for year 4 forever. The levels for year 4 and the number of graduating seniors are *output variables*.

You have now gone as far as you would want to go by

hand. With a computer you could (1) compensate for the fact that attrition rates are not as precise as previously indicated (by using the average and the variability of these rates), (2) include the effects of transfers in and out and other minor processes, and (3) modify some of the rates to determine what effects a particularly good or bad year would have on the total student population. Other inputs might occur to someone familiar with the processes that determine a college's size. The importance of proper inputs suggests that basic responsibility for any simulation ought to rest with someone familiar with the processes being simulated; knowledge of the structure and style of the simulation is less necessary.

Another use for simulation is to determine how different approaches will affect different operations. For example, how would the introduction of a second round of publicity handouts affect the rally schedule discussed in Chapter 9? It is *not* the case that, because we make them up, simulations contain no surprises. In fact, because we are simulating systems in which one factor can affect another, not only directly but through several different paths, we ought to expect some surprises. Jay Forrester, who has developed several complex systems simulations including *Urban Dynamics* (1969), states that virtually all of the consequences of specific changes in a system are unanticipated either in degree or direction. For example, his urban simulation revealed that a program to build low income housing might well result in a greater housing shortage after five years than existed when the program began. You will find, if you do a simulation, that the surprises may be either built into the system (e.g., a random number generator to approximate the output of some process) or simply the product of the way we have joined variables into complex patterns, but there will almost always be surprises.

RULE 10.1   *a*) Successful simulation requires that you have easy access to relevant data.

 b) Any part of a simulation may be built in any order. Once you begin building a part, however, test it and make certain it works properly be-

fore building another part. Connect the parts
only after you are certain that each individual
part works.

c) Keep each part of your model simple and understandable.

Simulations indicate how an alternative or provisional theory will operate under certain ranges of values for variables.
They allow us to test values for variables close to the beginning of a theory (which have the greatest effect on the theory), an obviously valuable function. If you have had formal
or symbolic logic, you will find that a theory composed of
dichotomous concepts with relations as specified in Chapter
4 may be simulated with a logical truth table.

Simulations are particularly susceptible to use as "magic,"
or "window dressing." Although they can be extremely useful in demonstrating the effects of changes, be wary of their
misuse. For example, the college simulation begun above
would be misused if someone actually started a college on the
basis of that simulation alone. A simulation should be checked
against any real data and experience that exists before it is
accepted. To take the numbers generated in Table 10.1 as
somehow "true" and "necessary" in and of themselves would
be to misuse them. To use these numbers without telling anyone how you got them would be to misuse them as "magic."
To use them saying something like the following: "The
mighty IBM computer, operating at lightning speeds, produced these numbers for our planning operation," would be
to misuse the simulation as "window dressing." You will
probably see many examples of simulation misuse during
your lifetime.

"PEOPLE" SIMULATIONS

A "people" simulation is undertaken when you have pieces
of a theory about how a process works but lack information
on how people will respond to the output of that process or
other pieces of input. People simulations are a cross between
games and simulations. For example, you may know how the

total population control program proposed in Chapter 8 would work, but you need to know how decision makers in different countries would respond to different kinds of programs. The situation is too complex to determine in factual detail what attributes (e.g., size, food supply) of the different countries might cause a decision maker to choose one program over another. It is also too complex to determine factually whether changing the presentation of any of the programs might affect acceptance rates. So you develop a people simulation in which persons are given appropriate information about "their" countries and play the roles of decision makers in those countries. Your task, then, is to interpret the outcome from many playing sessions and infer from that information what the real decision makers are likely to do.

People simulations are used in business situations (e.g., marketing, finance, production), international relations (e.g., war, diplomacy), bureaucratic decision making, and land use and development. See this chapter's Bibliography for references to some of these simulations.

RULE 10.2 *a)* People simulations are most useful when the role of each participant is clearly defined and time is given to role explanations.

   b) The simulation's output to its players should be easily understandable and reasonable.

GAMES

In games, the rule maker determines some processes and the players determine others, usually to a greater degree than in people simulation. A game must include (1) specific goals, (2) manipulatable variables, (3) a balance of control, and (4) resource exchange.

A game's goal can be either to teach or to experiment. If you want to teach a concept (e.g., balance of power, labor market behavior, or task leadership in a small group) or skill (e.g., bargaining, verbal presentation, or bluffing) or acquaint participants with the difficulties of decision making under pressure, your basic objective is to teach. If, however, your purpose is to learn how people act under certain kinds of pressure, determine probabilities for decision trees, or examine alternatives or turning points in certain crucial events, then your purpose is basically experimental. These objectives tend to remove pure games of chance from our consideration although many of us have "learned" the very real effects of chance through card and dice games.

Second, your game must be modeled in terms that contain some manipulatable variables (e.g., the situation, the process, or the system being "gamed"). You therefore need a prototheory. Parts of this prototheory can be "gamed" to see what values of what variables are likely under certain conditions, or to see whether the concepts used are sufficient to explain the outcomes in a game situation. In such cases the game becomes an experiment. You should probably try not to maximize both the teaching and the experimental aspects in a game. One part of your prototheory should state those activities which the players will be permitted to perform (i.e., the rules governing players' behavior). A second part should include responses from the environment (e.g., the bank, the judge, other players, the rules) when certain activities are performed.

You must also determine the balance of control (access to the manipulatable variables that affect the outcomes of each play) to be distributed among a first player, other players, and some set of random (or semirandom) events. This balance of control established by the rules regulates the flow of resources (rewards) from one player to another. Table 10.2 shows games in which different balances of access occur.

Table 10.2 The Balance of Control

Game	First Player Control	Other Player Control	Environmental Responses
Basketball foul shooting (alone)	X		
Class or fencing match	X	X	
Monopoly	X	X	X
Craps (played honestly)			X
Solitary games	X		X

Finally, you must determine the resources that players exchange or collect in competition with other players. Often these resources are given precise values so that success or failure can be evaluated after the game. The resource exchange should relate to the game's specific objective; there must also be clear objectives to the acts of trading themselves. Such resources can be money, points, prestige, and so on.

TEACHING GAMES

James Coleman's *Game of Democracy*, Part I, "The Legislative Session," exemplifies a game in which teaching goals are maximized. Coleman's objective is to teach the player the kinds of pressures under which a legislator operates. He does this by giving each player information on his "constituents'" preferences and then having a reelection (or not) determine the winner (loser). This arrangement pressures the "legislator" into making "deals" on issues that his constituents care little about in order to obtain votes on issues important to them. Coleman describes this arrangement:

> Each player—who is now a Legislator—receives a series of cards. Each card indicates the preferences of some voters in his constituency on one issue, and the set of cards he receives indicates the preferences of all voters in the Legislator's constituency. This gives him certain preferences or interests toward which he must work; these may not be his own preferences but are those of his constituents. At the end of the Legislative Session, each Legislator counts up the total number of constituents' votes in his favor and the total number against him, taken from the numbers on his constituency cards. This is his final score and represents how well he has satisfied his constituents, and in turn, received their votes for his re-election. Adding up the scores for all Legislators shows the overall satisfaction that this Legislature has given to the citizens of the society they represent. If this score is positive, there is a net positive satisfaction resulting from the legislative decisions. If it

is a negative, there is a dissatisfied electorate. [Coleman, 1966, p. 6]

When deals are made, the results are usually a reelected legislative body and a more satisfied "electorate." This game teaches players one aspect of how the legislative system works. Some aspects, of course (seniority, lobbying, etc.) are not included.

EXPERIMENTAL GAMES

You might use a game rather than a simulation if you have gaps in your prototheory and need some alternative experiences to consider as sources of concepts to fill those gaps.

One standard game exemplifying experimental use is called the "Prisoners' Dilemma."[1] The game begins with the capture of two suspects in a criminal case. The prosecutor separates the prisoners and begins to question them. Lacking evidence to convict either prisoner unless one of them confesses, the prosecutor proposes a deal to each of them separately: "If you will confess and implicate your partner, I will suggest that you be given a lesser penalty as a reward for cooperating with the state." The "hooker" in the deal is that if both confess, then the prosecutor will not need all the evidence, and he is likely to request a severe penalty for both. Table 10.3 depicts the alternatives. The dilemma is that either prisoner can gain his freedom only by talking; but if he talks and his accomplice also talks, then they will both receive longer sentences than if they had remained silent. Will they trust one another sufficiently to keep quiet?

Table 10.3 Outcomes of Prisoners' Dilemma Game

| | | Prisoner B | |
		Keeps Silent	Talks
Prisoner A	Keeps Silent	A: 1 year B: 1 year	A: 10 years B: Free
	Talks	A: Free B: 10 years	A: 5 years B: 5 years

[1] This discussion based on Rapoport (1960).

This game has been used as an empirical situation for the concept "trust." Attempts have also been made to predict, from psychological tests and previous histories of the pair of people playing the game, what their responses to this situation will be. Interests of humanity suggest that this game not be played experimentally with real prisoners. If the reward is changed from time off to money, however, it can be, and often is, played by volunteers.

In sum, the prisoners' dilemma situation and other competitive and cooperative games which incorporate a payoff of some variety are often played because a theorist needs experiences to help him determine how personality, distribution of rewards, information about a situation, and so on affect the way in which people play a game. These games can be played by two or more parties thus introducing coalition effects, personality interactions, and the further development of rules for the game.

RULE 10.3 *a*) Outline your objective for the game.

b) Build a simple model of the game's process.

c) Outline the rules.

d) Establish resources to be exchanged and objectives for exchange, and relate these two factors to the general purpose of the game.

e) Evaluate the balance of control.

SUMMARY

In this chapter we have examined two techniques, simulations and games, that use theory. Simulations are useful when we know many parts of a complex system but do not understand how they will operate when connected into that complex system. Games are most useful when we want to teach some aspect of social life or need to know how people will respond to different situations.

You can use the suggestions in this chapter to begin building a simple simulation or game. You will probably need professional help, however, as you encounter difficulties specific to your particular project. In fact:

RULE 10.4 If you encounter difficulties in building either a simple simulation or game, seek professional help. Do not expect perfection on your first effort.

These last three chapters have discussed models, plans, simulations and games largely as practical ways to use theory. But you should also know that each is a potential source for *new* theory-building efforts, reestablishing the building, testing, and theory-using cycle.

RULE 10.5 Use your models, plans, simulations, and games as sources for new theory-building efforts.

RULES

RULE 10.1 *a)* Successful simulation requires that you have easy access to relevant data.

b) Any part of a simulation may be built in any order. Once you begin building a part, however, test it and make certain it works properly before building another part. Connect the parts only after you are certain that each individual part works.

c) Keep each part of your model simple and understandable.

RULE 10.2 *a)* People simulations are most useful when the role of each participant is clearly defined and time is given to role explanations.

b) The simulation's output to its players should be easily understandable and reasonable.

RULE 10.3 *a)* Outline your objective for the game.

b) Build a simple model of the game's process.

c) Outline the rules.

d) Establish resources to be exchanged and objectives for exchange, and relate these two factors to the general purpose of the game.

e) Evaluate the balance of control.

RULE 10.4 If you encounter difficulties in building either a simple simulation or game, seek professional help. Do not expect perfection on your first effort.

RULE 10.5 Use your models, plans, simulations, and games as sources for new theory-building efforts.

EXERCISES

1. Simulate some small part of your college scene (e.g., dining hall or snack bar lines, hiring and firing, dormitory room assignments, course enrollments, student organization turnover, degree requirements) that you know something about or have learned something about this term. State some reasonable values for the variables in your model; you will not be asked to justify their accuracy. Finally, indicate your control variables, fixed variables, intermediate values, and output variables.
2. If you have studied logic, use a logical truth table to simulate a provisional theory containing nothing but dichotomous concepts.
3. Develop a game. Describe it. Report:
    a) The balance among first party control, second party control, and random factors;
    b) The set of rules, and indicate lines that play might follow;
    c) The possible outcomes (who wins and how you tell);
    d) The outcome (play it at least once). What needs improving? Is it playable?
    e) What it teaches or what you learned.

BIBLIOGRAPHY

ABT, CLARK C. *Serious Games*. New York: The Viking Press, 1970.

A serious discussion of teaching games. Includes many examples.

COLEMAN, JAMES. *The Game of Democracy*. Washington, D.C.: National 4-H Club Foundation, 1966.

Another example of a teaching game.

FORRESTER, JAY W. *Urban Dynamics*. Cambridge, Mass.: The MIT Press, 1969.

A simulation of urban growth and decay.

GAMSON, WILLIAM. *SIMSOC: Simulated Society*. New York: The Free Press, 1969.

A people simulation of a society.

GUETZKOW, HAROLD, and CLEO H. CHERRYHOLMES. *Inter-Nation Simulation*. Chicago: Science Research Associates, 1966.

A people simulation of international relations.

RAPOPORT, ANATOL. *Fights, Games, and Debates*. Ann Arbor: University of Michigan Press, 1960.

An introduction to the analysis of concepts through experimental games.

RASER, JOHN R. *Simulation and Society: An Exploration of Scientific Gaming*. Boston: Allyn and Bacon, Inc., 1969.

A discussion of simulation and games, with emphasis on experimental games.

TOCHER, K. D. *The Art of Simulation*. London: The English Universities Press, 1963.

A technical but clear description of the process for writing simulations of production processes which might serve as models for social processes.

WEINBAUM, MARVIN G., and LOUIS H. GOLD. *Presidential Election*. New York: Holt, Rinehart and Winston, 1969.

A people simulation of an election.

BIBLIOGRAPHY

ABT, CLARK C. *Serious Games*. New York: The Viking Press, 1970.

ACKOFF, RUSSELL L. *Scientific Method: Optimizing Applied Research Decisions*. New York: John Wiley & Sons, Inc., 1962.

ACKOFF, RUSSELL L., and MAURICE SASIENI. *Fundamentals of Operations Research*. New York: John Wiley & Sons, Inc., 1968.

BARTOS, O. *Simple Models of Group Behavior*. New York: Columbia University Press, 1967.

BATTERSBY, ALBERT. *Mathematics in Management*. Baltimore, Md.: Penguin Books, 1966.

BERELSON, BERNARD, and GARY A. STEINER. *Human Behavior: An Inventory of Scientific Findings*. New York: Harcourt Brace Jovanovich, Inc., 1964.

BERGER, P., and T. LUCKMANN. *The Social Construction of Reality*. Garden City, N.Y.: Anchor Books, 1967.

BLALOCK, HUBERT. *Causal Inferences in Nonexperimental Research*. Chapel Hill: University of North Carolina Press, 1964.

BLALOCK, HUBERT. "Theory Building and Causal Inferences." In Hubert and Ann Blalock (eds.), *Methodology in Social Research*. New York: McGraw-Hill Book Company, 1968.

BLALOCK, HUBERT. "The Measurement Problem: A Gap Between the Languages of Theory and Research. In Hubert and Ann Blalock (eds.), *Methodology in Social Research*. New York: McGraw-Hill Book Company, 1968.

BLALOCK, HUBERT. *Theory Construction: From Verbal to Mathematical Formulations*. Englewood Cliffs, N.J.: Prentice-Hall, Inc., 1969.

BLALOCK, HUBERT. *An Introduction to Social Research*. Englewood Cliffs, N.J.: Prentice-Hall, Inc., 1970.

BLAU, PETER M., and OTIS DUDLEY DUNCAN. *The American Occupational Structure*. New York: John Wiley & Sons, Inc., 1967.

BOGUE, DONALD J. *Principles of Demography*. New York: John Wiley & Sons, Inc., 1969.

BOOCOCK, SARANE S., and E. O. SCHILD. *Simulation Games in Learning*. Beverly Hills: Sage Publications, Inc., 1968.

BRIGHT, MARGARET, GEORGE E. IMMERWAHR, and MELVIN ZELNIK. *Demographic Analysis*. Mimeographed. Baltimore: The Johns Hopkins University, June 1969.

BROSS, IRWIN D. J. *Design for Decision: An Introduction to Statistical Decision Making*. New York: The Free Press, 1965.

BUCKLEY, WALTER. *Sociology and Modern Systems Theory*. Englewood Cliffs, N.J.: Prentice-Hall, Inc., 1967.

BUNGE, MARIO. *The Myth of Simplicity: Problems of Scientific Philosophy*. Englewood Cliffs, N.J.: Prentice-Hall, Inc., 1963.

BUNGE, MARIO. *Scientific Research*. New York: Springer-Verlag, 1967.

CAMPBELL, NORMAN. *What Is Science?* New York: Dover Publications, Inc., 1952.

CARLSON, ELLIOT. *Learning Through Games*. Washington: Public Affairs Press, 1969.

CHURCH, ALONZO. *Introduction to Mathematical Logic*. Princeton, N.J.: Princton University Press, 1956.

CICOUREL, AARON V. *Method and Measurement in Sociology.* New York: The Free Press, 1964.

CLARK, KENNETH B., and JEANNETTE HOPKINS. *A Relevant War Against Poverty: A Study of Community Action Programs and Observable Social Change.* New York: Harper & Row, 1970.

COLEMAN, JAMES. *The Game of Democracy.* Washington, D.C.: National 4-H Club Federation, 1966.

DAVIS, JAMES A. *Study Design and Data Analysis in Sociology.* Englewood Cliffs, N.J.: Prentice-Hall, Inc., 1971.

DEUTSCH, MORTON. "Trust and Suspicion." *Journal of Conflict Resolution* (Dec. 1958), pp. 265–279.

DORN, HAROLD F. "Pitfalls in Population Forecasts and Projections." *Journal of the American Statistical Association,* 45 (Sept. 1950), 311–334.

DOWNS, ANTHONY. *Inside Bureaucracy.* Boston: Little, Brown and Company, 1967.

DUNCAN, OTIS DUDLEY. "Path Analysis: Sociological Examples." *American Journal of Sociology,* 72 (July 1966), 1–16.

ELLIS, BRIAN. *Basic Concepts of Measurement.* Cambridge: Cambridge University Press, 1968.

EWING, DAVID W. *The Practice of Planning.* New York: Harper & Row, 1968.

FAIRWEATHER, GEORGE. *Methods for Experimental Social Innovation.* New York: John Wiley & Sons, Inc., 1967.

FORRESTER, JAY W. *Urban Dynamics.* Cambridge, Mass.: The MIT Press, 1969.

GAMSON, WILLIAM. *SIMSOC: Simulated Society.* New York: The Free Press, 1969.

GARDNER, M. "Simplicity As a Scientific Concept: Does Nature Keep Her Accounts on a Thumbnail?" *Scientific American* (Aug. 1969), pp. 118–120.

GEERTZ, CLIFFORD. *The Religion of Java.* New York: The Free Press, 1964.

GOODMAN, LEO A., and WILLIAM H. KRUSKAL. "Measures of Association for Cross Classifications." *Journal of American Statistical Association,* 49 (Dec. 1954), 732–764.

GORDEN, RAYMOND L. *Interviewing: Strategy, Techniques and Tactics.* Homewood, Ill.: The Dorsey Press, 1969.

GREER, SCOTT. *The Logic of Social Inquiry.* Chicago: Aldine, 1969.

GUETZKOW, HAROLD, and CLEO H. CHERRYHOLMES. *Inter-Nation Simulation.* Chicago: Science Research Associates, 1966.

HANSON, NORWOOD RUSSELL. *Patterns of Discovery.* Cambridge: Cambridge University Press, 1958.

HARARY, FRANK, ROBERT Z. NORMAN, and DORWIN CARTWRIGHT. *Structural Models: An Introduction to the Theory of Directed Graphs.* New York: John Wiley & Sons, Inc., 1965.

HOMANS, GEORGE. *The Human Group.* New York: Harcourt Brace Jovanovich, Inc., 1950.

HOULT, THOMAS FORD. *Dictionary of Modern Sociology.* Totowa, N.J.: Littlefield, Adams and Co., 1969.

HUGGINS, W. H., and DORIS R. ENTWISLE. *Introductory Systems and Design.* Waltham, Mass.: Blaisdell Publishing Company, 1968.

JAFFE, A. J. *Handbook of Statistical Methods for Demographers.* Washington, D.C.: Government Printing Office, 1951.

KAHN, ALFRED J. *Studies in Social Policy and Planning.* New York: Russell Sage Foundation, 1969.

KAHN, ALFRED J. *Theory and Practice of Social Planning.* New York: Russell Sage Foundation, 1969.

KAPLAN, ABRAHAM. *The Conduct of Inquiry: Methodology for Behavioral Science.* San Francisco: Chandler Publishing Co., 1964.

KELLER, SUZANNE. *Beyond the Ruling Class: Strategic Elites in Modern Society.* New York: Random House, 1963.

KEMENY, JOHN G., J. LAURIE SNELL, and GERALD L. THOMPSON. *Introduction to Finite Mathematics*. 2d ed. Englewood Cliffs, N.J.: Prentice-Hall, Inc., 1966.

KENDALL, PATRICIA L., and PAUL LAZARSFELD. "Problems of Survey Analysis." In Robert K. Merton and Paul F. Lazarsfeld, *Continuities in Social Research*. New York: The Free Press, 1950.

KERLINGER, FRED N. *Foundations of Behavioral Research*. New York: Holt, Rinehart and Winston, 1966.

LEWIS, OSCAR. *Five Families: Mexican Case Studies in the Culture of Poverty*. New York: Mentor Books, 1959.

LIEBOW, ELLIOT. *Tally's Corner*. Boston: Little, Brown and Company, 1967.

MARCH, JAMES G., and HERBERT A. SIMON. *Organizations*. New York: John Wiley & Sons, Inc., 1958.

MARCUSE, HERBERT. *Eros and Civilization: A Philosophical Inquiry into Freud*. New York: Vintage Books, 1962.

MC CAIN, GARVIN, and ERWIN M. SEGAL. *The Game of Science*. Belmont, Calif.: Brooks/Cole Publishing Co., 1969.

MILLER, DELBERT C. *Handbook of Research Design and Social Measurement*, 2d ed. New York: David McKay Co., Inc., 1970.

MOYNIHAN, DANIEL P. *Maximum Feasible Misunderstanding*. New York: The Free Press, 1969.

MUELLER, JOHN H., KARL F. SCHUESSLER, and HERBERT L. COSTNER. *Statistical Reasoning in Sociology*. Boston: Houghton Mifflin Co., 1970.

MYRDAL, JAN. *Report from a Chinese Village*. New York: Signet Books, 1965.

New York Times Index. Serial. New York: The New York Times Co.

NATIONAL SCIENCE FOUNDATION. *American Science Manpower 1966.* Washington, D.C.: National Science Foundation, NSF 68–7, 1968, p. 92.

ORCUTT, GUY, ALICE M. RIVLIN, MARTIN GREENBERGER, and JOHN KORBEL. *Microanalysis of Socio-Economic Systems.* New York: Harper & Row, 1961.

PARSONS, TALCOTT. *Societies: Evolutionary and Comparative Perspectives.* Englewood Cliffs, N.J.: Prentice-Hall, Inc., 1966.

PHILLIPS, BERNARD S. *Social Research: Strategy and Tactics.* New York: The Macmillan Company, 1966.

RAPOPORT, ANATOL. *Fights, Games and Debates.* Ann Arbor: University of Michigan Press, 1960.

RAPPORT, SAMUEL, and HELEN WRIGHT. *Science: Method and Meaning.* New York: New York University Press, 1963.

RASER, JOHN R. *Simulation and Society: An Exploration of Scientific Gaming.* Boston: Allyn and Bacon, Inc., 1969.
Reader's Guide to Periodical Literature. Serial. New York, H. W. Wilson Co.

SCHRAG, C. "Elements of Theoretical Analysis in Sociology." In L. Gross, *Sociological Theories: Inquiries and Paradigms.* New York: Harper & Row, 1967.

SELLTIZ, CLAIRE, MARIE JAHODA, MORTON DEUTSCH, and STUART W. COOK. *Research Methods in Social Relations.* Rev. 1-vol. ed. New York: Holt, Rinehart and Winston, 1966.

SIEGEL, SIDNEY. *Nonparametric Statistics for the Behavioral Sciences.* New York: McGraw-Hill Book Company, 1956.

SILLS, DAVID L. (ed.). *International Encyclopedia of the Social Sciences.* New York: The Macmillan Company and The Free Press, 1968.

SIMON, HERBERT (ed.). *Models of Man.* New York: John Wiley & Sons, Inc., 1957.

SIMON, JULIAN L. *Basic Research Methods in Social Science: The Art of Empirical Investigation*. New York: Random House, 1969.

SOLZHENITSYN, ALEXSANDR L. *The First Circle*. New York: Bantam Books, 1969.

STINCHCOMBE, ARTHUR. *Constructing Social Theories*. New York: Harcourt Brace Jovanovich, Inc., 1968.

SUCHMAN, E. *Evaluative Research*. New York: Russell Sage Foundation, 1967.

TOCHER, K. D. *The Art of Simulation*. London: The English Universities Press, 1963.

U.S. BUREAU OF THE CENSUS. *Statistical Abstract of the United States: 1970*. Washington, D.C.: Government Printing Office, 1970.

WEBB, EUGENE J., DONALD T. CAMPBELL, RICHARD D. SCHWARTZ, and LEE SECHREST. *Unobtrusive Measures: Nonreactive Research in the Social Sciences*. Chicago: Rand McNally and Co., 1966.

Webster's New Dictionary of Synonyms. Springfield, Mass.: G. and C. Merriam Co., 1968.

Webster's Third New International Dictionary. Philip B. Gove (ed.). Springfield, Mass.: G. and C. Merriam Co., 1964.

WEINBAUM, MARVIN G., and LOUIS H. GOLD. *Presidential Election*. New York: Holt, Rinehart and Winston, 1969.

WOLD, HERMAN, and LARS JUREEN. *Demand Analysis*. New York: John Wiley & Sons, Inc., 1953.

WRIGHT, SEWALL. "The Method of Path Coefficients." *Annals of Mathematical Statistics*, 5 (Sept. 1934), 161–215.

WRIGHT, SEWALL. "The Interpretation of Multivariate Systems." In O. Kempthorne, *et al.* (eds.), *Statistics and Mathematics in Biology*. Ames: Iowa State College Press, 1954.

ZETTERBERG, HANS. *On Theory and Verification in Sociology*. Totowa, N.J.: The Bedminster Press, 1963.

ZIMAN, JOHN. *Public Knowledge: The Social Dimension of Science*. Cambridge: Cambridge University Press, 1968.

INDEX

71 72 73 74 7 6 5 4 3 2 1